presentationzen

Simple ideas on presentation design and delivery

New Riders

Garr Reynolds

Presentation Zen: Simple Ideas on Presentation Design and Delivery
Garr Reynolds

New Riders
1249 Eighth Street
Berkeley, CA 94710
510/524-2178
510/524-2221 (fax)

Find us on the Web at: www.newriders.com
To report errors, please send a note to errata@peachpit.com

New Riders is an imprint of Peachpit, a division of Pearson Education

Project Editor: Michael J. Nolan
Development Editor: Marta Justak
Production Editor: Hilal Sala
Proofreader: Rose Weisburd
Indexer: Julie Bess
Design Consultant in Japan: Mayumi Nakamoto
Book design: Garr Reynolds

ISBN 13: 978-0-321-52565-9
ISBN 10: 0-321-52565-5

9

Printed and bound in the United States of America

To Mom & Dad

Table of Contents

Acknowledgments

This book would not have been possible without a lot of help and support. I'd like to thank the following people for their contributions and encouragement:

Nancy Duarte and Mark Duarte and all the kick-butt staff at Duarte Design in Silicon Valley, including Victoria Davis, Trish Gilfoil, and Paula Tesch for their constant support.

At New Riders: Michael Nolan (Project Editor), who asked me to write this book and gave me the freedom to do it my way (yeah, like the song). Marta Justak (Development Editor), who was amazing at bringing more clarity to my writing. Rose Weisburd (Proofreader), who has magical powers for finding errors and offering advice for making the writing better. Mimi Heft for her help with the design and the cover. Hilal Sala (Production Editor) for her talent and great patience.

Guy Kawasaki, Seth Godin, David S. Rose, Daniel Pink, Dan Heath and Rick Heath, Rosamund Zander, Jim Quirk, Deryn Verity for their enlightened advice and content in the early stages of the process.

Garth Johnson and all the cool people at iStockphoto.com for their tremendous support with the images and the special offer that's included at the back of this book.

Designer Mayumi Nakamoto for teaching me more than I wanted to know (or thought possible) about Adobe InDesign. June Cohen and Michael Glass at TED for their help with the images. Daniel Lee at Mojo for his help with the credits. Aaron Walker, Tom Grant's producer in Japan, for his great assistance.

The Design Matters Japan community including Toru Yamada, Shigeki Yamamoto, Tom Perry, Darren Saunders, Daniel Rodriguez, Kjeld Duits, David Baldwin, Nathan Bryan, Jiri Mestecky, Doug Schafer, Barry Louie, and many, many others.

Back in the States, a big thank you to those who contributed ideas and support including Debbie Thorn, CZ Robertson, David Roemer, and Gail Murphy. And to Mark and Liz Reynolds for their fantastic B&B at the beach.

I'd like to thank the thousands of subscribers to the Presentation Zen blog and to all the blog readers who have contacted me over the years to share their stories and examples, especially Les Posen in Australia.

Though I could not include all the slides in this book, I want to thank all the people who submitted sample slides including: Jeff Brenman, Chris Landry, Scott B. Schwertly, Jill Cadarette, Kelli Matthews, Luis Iturriaga, Dr. Aisyah Saad Abdul Rahim, Marty Neumeier, Markuz Wernli Saito, Sangeeta Kumar, Allysson Lucca, Pam Slim, Jed Schmidt, Merlin Mann, and many others.

And of course my biggest supporter in all of this was my wife, Ai, who was always understanding and a great source of inspiration and ideas (and occasionally, chocolate chip cookies).

Foreword by Guy Kawasaki

Since this is a book about presenting better with slides, I thought it would be appropriate to show the foreword as a slide presentation. As far as I know, this is the first foreword in history presented in a book as a series of PowerPoint slides. Now, good slides should *enhance* a live talk; slides are not meant to tell the whole story without you there. But from these slides on the next page I think you can get my point. If I were to give a live talk about why you should buy this book, the slides would look something like this.

Guy Kawasaki
Managing Director,
Garage Technology Ventures
Co-founder of Truemors
www.guykawasaki.com

FOREWORD for Presentation Zen

Guy Kawasaki
Managing Director,
Garage Technology Ventures
Co-founder of Truemors
Garage | Truemors

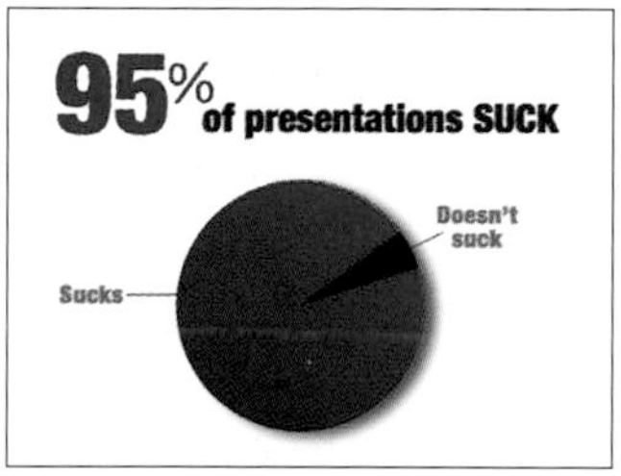

95% of presentations SUCK

Doesn't suck

Sucks

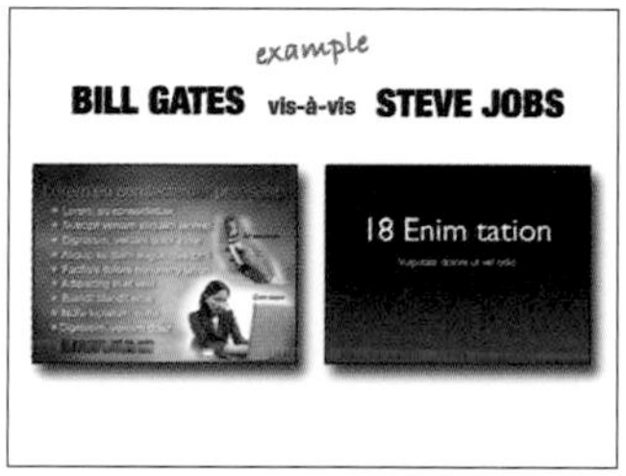

---

example
BILL GATES vis-à-vis **STEVE JOBS**

18 Enim tation

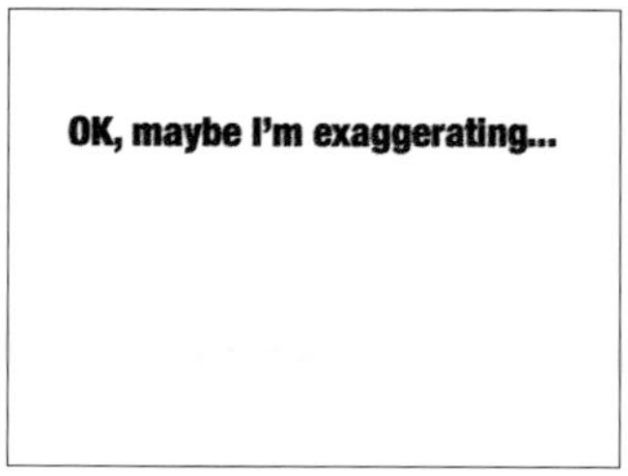

OK, maybe I'm exaggerating...

It's actually **99**%

Doesn't suck

Sucks

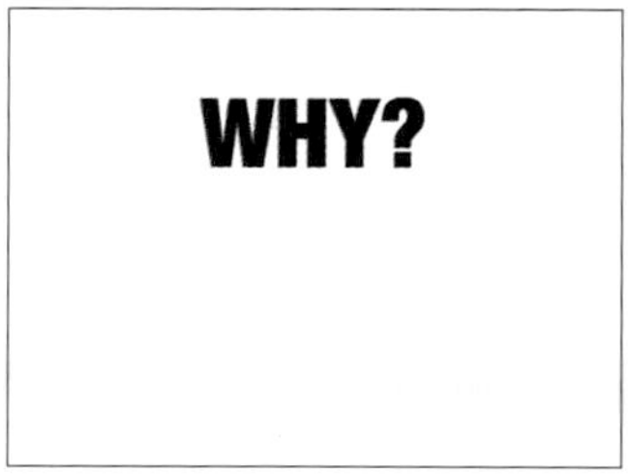

WHY?

What we see:
Long
Boring
Bad slides
Content-free

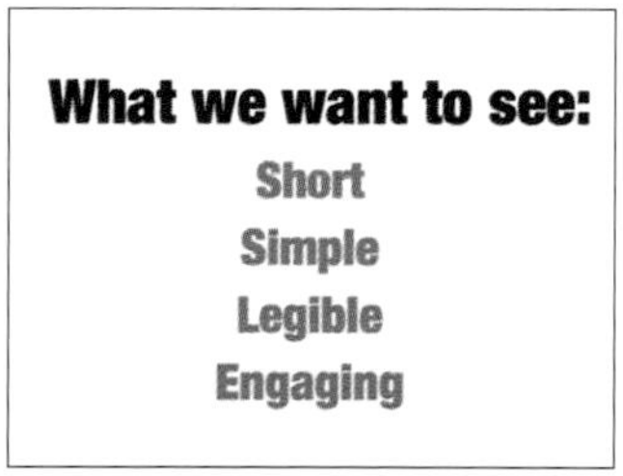

What we want to see:
Short
Simple
Legible
Engaging

BUT...

Houston, we have a problem!

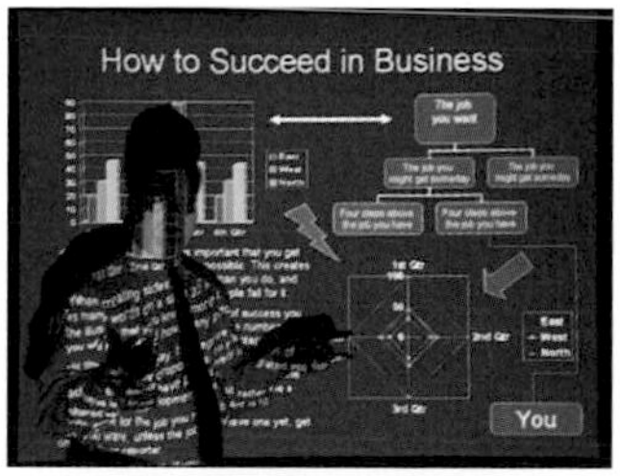

How to Succeed in Business

THIS BOOK IS YOUR SOLUTION

presentation zen
Garr Reynolds

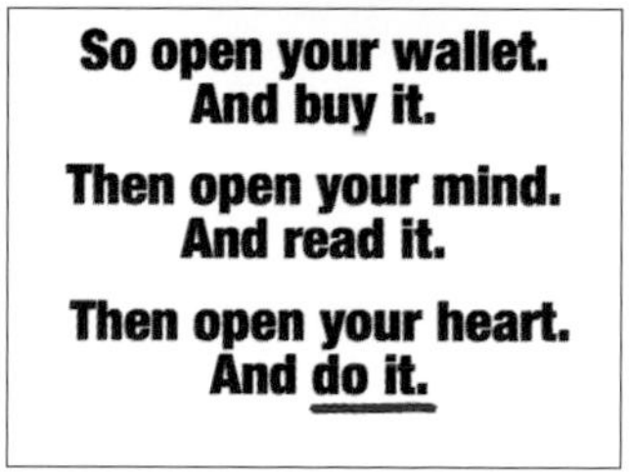

So open your wallet. And buy it.

Then open your mind. And read it.

Then open your heart. And do it.

THANK YOU!

Guy Kawasaki

introduction

Simplicity is the ultimate sophistication.

— Leonardo da Vinci

Presenting in Today's World

With successful presentations in Tokyo behind me, I boarded the 5:03pm Super Express bound for Osaka complete with my *ekiben* (a special kind of Japanese lunch box or *bento* sold at train stations) and a can of Asahi beer in hand. The quintessential "Japan experience" for me is zipping through the Japanese countryside aboard cutting-edge rail technology while sampling traditional Japanese delicacies with my chopsticks, sipping Japanese beer, and catching glimpses of temples, shrines, and even Mount Fuji out the spacious side window. It's a wonderful juxtaposition of the old and the new, and a pleasant way to end the day.

While in the midst of savoring the contents of my bento, I glanced to my right across the aisle to see a Japanese businessman with a pensive look on his face reviewing a printed deck of PowerPoint slides. Two slides per page, one page after another filled with boxes crammed with reams of Japanese text in several different colors. No empty space. No graphics except for the company logo at the top of each slide box. Just slide after slide of text, subject titles, bullet points, and logos.

Were these slides used for visual support in a live oral presentation? If so, I sympathize with the audience. Since when can an audience read and listen to someone talk at the same time (even if they could actually see the 12-point text on the screen well enough to read it)? Were the slides used merely as a kind of document printed in PowerPoint? If so, I pity both the author and the reader because PowerPoint is not a tool for document creation. Boxes of bullet points and logos do not make for a good handout or report. And judging by the way the man was flipping back and forth between the printed slides, perhaps frustrated by the ambiguity of the content, this was becoming apparent to him.

What a contrast in the presentation of content, I thought to myself: The beautifully efficient, well-designed Japanese bento before me containing nothing superfluous, compared with the poorly-designed, difficult-to-understand deck of printed PowerPoint slides across the aisle. Why couldn't the design and presentation of business and technical content for a live talk have more in common with the spirit of the simple bentos sold at Japanese train stations? For example, the Japanese bento contains appropriate content arranged in the most efficient, graceful manner. The bento is presented in a simple, beautiful, and balanced way. Nothing lacking. Nothing superfluous. Not decorated, but wonderfully designed. It looks good, and it tastes good. A satisfying, inspiring, and fulfilling way to spend 20 minutes. When was the last time you could say the same about a presentation?

A delicious Japanese bento and a PowerPoint presentation may seem to have nothing in common, but it was at that moment in time many years ago, rolling across Japan at 200 miles an hour, that I had an insight or an "awakening." With this flash of awareness, I realized that something needed to be done to end the scourge of bad PowerPoint slides and the lifeless narration that accompanies them, and that I could do something to help. In Japan, just like everywhere else in the world, professionals suffer through poorly designed presentations on a daily basis. Presentations in which the slides often do more harm than good. It is not enjoyable, and it is not effective. I knew that if I could begin to help others look at preparation, design, and delivery of so-called "PowerPoint presentations" in a different way, perhaps I could do my small part to help others communicate far more effectively. That moment on the Bullet Train—somewhere between Yokohama and Nagoya—was when I began writing this book by sharing my thoughts on the Presentation Zen Web site, a blog that would go on to become the most visited site on presentation design on the net.

This book has three sections: Preparation, Design, and Delivery. Along the way I'll provide a good balance of principles and concepts, inspiration, and practical examples. I'll even show you before/after photos of the actual bento on the Bullet Train that was the inspiration for this book. Before reviewing the current state of presentations today and why presentations matter now more than ever before, let's first look at what is meant by "Presentation Zen."

The Presentation Zen Approach

This is not a book about Zen; this is a book about communication and about seeing presentations in a slightly different way, a way that is in tune with our times. Although I make several references to Zen and the Zen arts along the way, my references to Zen are far more in the realm of an analogy, rather than being literal. Literally, the tradition of Zen or Zen practice has nothing to do directly with "the art" of presenting in today's world. However, our professional activities—especially professional communications—can share the same ethos as Zen. That is, the essence or the spirit of many of the principles found in Zen concerning aesthetics, mindfulness, connectedness, and so on can be applied to our daily activities, including presentations.

A teacher for one who seeks enlightenment would say that the first step for the student is to truly see that life is somehow out of sync or off-kilter, that there is "suffering" if you will. And that this "out-of-kilterness" is a consequence of our own attachment to things that are inconsequential. Likewise, the first step to creating and designing great presentations is to be mindful of the current state of what passes for "normal" PowerPoint presentations and that what is "normal" today is out of sync and off-kilter with how people actually learn and communicate.

Each situation is different. But we all know, through our own experience, that the current state of presentations in business and academia causes its own degree of "suffering" for audiences and for presenters alike. If we desire to communicate with more clarity, integrity, beauty, and intelligence, then we must move beyond what is considered to be "normal" to something different and far more effective. The principles I am most mindful of through every step of the presentation process are restraint, simplicity, and naturalness: Restraint in preparation. Simplicity in design. Naturalness in delivery. All of which, in the end, lead to greater clarity for us and for our audience.

In many ways, few of the basics have changed since the time of Aristotle some 2300 years ago, or from the basic advice given by Dale Carnegie in the 1930s. But what may seem like common sense regarding presentations is not common practice. The Presentation Zen approach challenges the conventional wisdom of making PowerPoint presentations in today's world and encourages people to think differently about the design, and delivery of their presentations.

An Approach, Not a Method

Presentation Zen, however, is not a method. Method implies a step-by-step systematic process, something very much planned and linear, with a definite proven procedure that you can pick off a shelf and follow A to Z in a logical orderly fashion. Presentation Zen, then, is more of an approach. An approach implies a road, a direction, a frame of mind, perhaps even a philosophy, but not a formula of proven rules to be followed. Methods are important and necessary. But there are no panaceas, and I offer no prescriptions for success. Success depends on you and your own unique situation. However, I do offer guidelines and some things to think about that may run contrary to conventional wisdom on how to make a live presentation with multimedia.

Similarly, Zen itself is an approach to life and a way of being, rather than a set of rules or dogma to be followed by all in the same way. Indeed, there are many paths to enlightenment. At the heart of Zen is the need for personal awareness and the ability to see and discover. Zen is practical and is concerned with the here and now. And the practical and the here and now is what we're concerned with here too with presentations. The aim of this book is to help professionals free themselves from the pain of creating and delivering presentations by helping them see presentations in a way that is different, simpler, more visual, more natural, and ultimately far more meaningful.

Each Case Is Different

Not all presentation situations are appropriate for using multimedia. For example, if you have a small audience and data-intensive materials to discuss, a handout of the materials with a give-and-take discussion is usually more appropriate. There are many situations when a whiteboard or flipcharts or a paper with detailed figures make for better support. Each case is different. The discussions in this book, however, center among those presentations when multimedia is a good fit with your unique situation.

This book is not directly about software tools. Yet, by keeping principles such as restraint and simplicity in mind, you can use the lessons here to help you design better visuals appropriate for your situation. When it comes to software functions, I don't think the challenge is to learn more, but rather to ignore more and forget more so that you can focus on the principles and the few techniques that are important. Software techniques are simply not our chief concern.

Characterizing master swordsman Odagiri Ichiun's ideas on technique, Zen scholar Daisetz Suzuki says, "...the first principle of the art is not to rely on tricks of technique. Most swordsmen make too much of technique, sometimes making it their chief concern..." And most presenters make the software their chief concern in the preparation process and in the delivery. This often ends up in cluttered visuals and cluttered talks that are neither engaging nor memorable.

Yes, the basics of software are important to know. Delivery techniques and "dos and don'ts" are useful to understand. But it's not about technique alone. The "art of presentation" transcends technique and enables an individual to remove walls and connect with an audience to inform or persuade in a very meaningful, unique moment in time.

Where We Are Today: Really Bad PowerPoint

It seems as if PowerPoint has been around forever, but in truth it's only been in common use for about 15–20 years. PowerPoint 1.0 was created in Silicon Valley in 1987 by Robert Gaskins and Dennis Austin as a way to display presentation images on a Mac. It was cool. And it worked. They sold the application later that year to Microsoft. A version for the PC would hit the market a couple years later, and (oy vey!) the world hasn't been the same since.

PowerPoint became popular in the 1990s, and by the year 2000 the use of the application was ubiquitous in businesses and schools across the globe. But all was not good. It was around this time, in fact, that the term "Death by PowerPoint" began to be tossed around. In 2001, marketing guru and best-selling author Seth Godin—who's seen more bad presentations than any man should be subjected to—had had enough. Seth decided he'd try to make a difference. So he wrote a 10-page e-book called *Really Bad PowerPoint* that he sold on Amazon for $2 (money went to charity), and it became the best-selling e-book of the year.

"PowerPoint could be the most powerful tool on your computer, but it's not," Seth said. "It's actually a dismal failure. Almost every PowerPoint presentation sucks rotten eggs." Visual communications guru Edward Tufte, who has written some wonderful books on the proper ways to display quantitative information, such as *Beautiful Evidence* and *Visual Explanations* (Graphics Press), joined the chorus of those deriding the PowerPoint tool in a September 2003 *Wired Magazine* article simply titled "PowerPoint Is Evil." "At a minimum," says Tufte, "a presentation format should do no harm. Yet the PowerPoint style routinely disrupts, dominates, and trivializes content. Thus PowerPoint presentations too often resemble a school play—very loud, very slow, and very simple."

Millions of presentations are now given every day with the aid of PowerPoint or other slideware.* Yet, most presentations remain mind-numbingly dull, something to be endured by both presenter and audience alike. Presentations

---

Slideware is a term, which to my knowledge, originated with Edward Tufte to describe PowerPoint and similar applications, such as Keynote.

are generally ineffective, not because presenters lack intelligence or creativity, but because they have learned bad habits and lack awareness and knowledge about what makes for a great presentation (and what does not). The typical slide presentation of today consists of a speaker presenting streams of in-formation to slides with general titles, clip art, and bulleted list after bulleted list in the all-too familiar topic/subtopic hierarchical format. Presenting with slides is so much apart of our culture now that people can hardly imagine preparing for a meeting and presenting at that meeting without slides.

The Scourge of the Deck

Conferences also have perpetuated the bullet-filled deck by asking presenters to follow a "standard slide format." Kathy Sierra, co-author of *Head First Java* (O'Reilly Media), as well as the Creating Passionate Users weblog, has attended and presented at a lot of conferences. Here's what she said on her website in 2005 in a post entitled "Stop your presentation before it kills again": "Given how many people hate slide presentations," Sierra says, "why is it universally assumed that where there is 'a talk,' there's PowerPoint (or its much cooler cousin, Apple's Keynote)? Conference coordinators rarely ask speakers if they'll be projecting slides. They send out the slide templates, then start demanding your slides several weeks before the show. Saying you don't have slides is like saying you'll give your talk naked." And what kind of "visuals" are people using to support their conference talks? "Visuals are more memorable than words, but bullet points are still the prevailing content of most slides, and they usually add nothing," says Sierra.

Is It Finally Time to Ditch PowerPoint?

In the spring of 2007, The Sydney Morning Herald ran an article entitled "Researcher points finger at PowerPoint," by Anna Patty, which generated quite a stir. The article highlighted findings by researchers from the University of New South Wales, including John Sweller, who developed the cognitive load theory in the 1980s. One of the findings mentioned in the article: it is more difficult to process information if it is coming at you both verbally and in written form at the same time. Since people cannot read and listen well at the same time, the reporter suggested, this might mean "the death of the PowerPoint presentation." The assumption being that a presentation made with the aid of slideware, such as PowerPoint or Keynote, must necessarily include lines of text projected on a screen that mirrors the spoken word of the presenter. The article generated a lot of attention, due in part to this quote by Professor Sweller:

> *"The use of the PowerPoint presentation has been a disaster.*
> *It should be ditched."*
> — *John Sweller*

Professor Sweller's comment makes a provocative headline and adds to the long list of professionals and researchers deriding the PowerPoint tool. What Professor Sweller surely means is that *the way* PowerPoint is used should be ditched. And with that I agree. There is some truth to the idea that the templates and all the bells and whistles added to PowerPoint through the years have contributed to some of the "really bad PowerPoint." But PowerPoint (or Keynote, etc.) is not a method; it is a tool that can be used effectively with appropriate design methods or ineffectively with inappropriate methods.

The Times They Are a-Changing

So, is it finally time to ditch PowerPoint? Hardly, but it is long past time to ditch the use of the ubiquitous bulleted-list templates found in both PowerPoint and Keynote. And it's long past time that we realized that putting the same information on a slide in text form that is coming out of our mouths usually does not help—in fact, it hurts our message. Most of us know intuitively that when we've got 20 minutes to make a presentation, presenting to an audience with a screen of text-filled slides does not work. Research supports the idea that it is indeed more difficult for audiences to process information when it is being presented to them in spoken and written form at the same time. So perhaps it would be better to just remain silent and let people read the slides. But this raises the issue: Why are you there?

A good oral presentation is different than a well-written document, and attempts to merge them result in poor presentations and poor documents. The bad news is that most oral presentations accompanied by multimedia are quite mediocre today. But the good news is that this is an opportunity for you to be different. The bar is pretty low now, so even improving in small steps may make a big difference. However, as more and more people realize that the "conventional wisdom" about presenting is out of sync with reality, expectations will surely rise.

Presentations in "The Conceptual Age"

My favorite book in the summer of 2006 was Daniel Pink's best-seller, *A Whole New Mind* (Riverhead Trade). Tom Peters called the book "a miracle." There's a reason. *A Whole New Mind* sets the context for the "Presentation Zen approach" to presenting in today's world, an era that Pink and others have dubbed "the conceptual age" where "high-touch" and "high-concept" aptitudes are first among equals. "The future belongs to a different kind of person," Pink says. "Designers, inventors, teachers, storytellers—creative and empathetic right-brain thinkers whose abilities mark the fault line between who gets ahead and who doesn't."

In *A Whole New Mind,* Pink paints an accurate and vivid picture of the threats and opportunities facing professionals today. Pink claims we're living in a different era, a different age. An age in which those who "Think different" will be valued even more than ever. We're living in an age, says Pink, that is "...animated by a different form of thinking and a new approach to life—one that prizes aptitudes that I call 'high concept' and 'high touch.' High concept involves the capacity to detect patterns and opportunities, to create artistic and emotional beauty, to craft a satisfying narrative...."

Now, Pink is not saying that logic and analysis (so-called "left-brain reasoning"), which are so important in "the information age," are not important in "the conceptual age" of today. Indeed, logical thinking is as important as it ever has been. So-called "right-brain reasoning" alone is not going to keep the space shuttle up or cure disease. Logical reasoning is a necessary condition. However, it's increasingly clear that logic alone is not a sufficient condition for success for individuals and for organizations. Right-brain thinking is every bit as important now—in some cases more important—than left-brain thinking. (The right-brain/left-brain distinction is a metaphor based on real differences between the two hemispheres; a healthy person uses both hemispheres for even simple tasks.)

Particularly valuable in *A Whole New Mind* are the "six senses" or the six "right-brain directed aptitudes," which Pink says are necessary for successful professionals to possess in the more interdependent world we live in, a world of increased automation and out-sourcing.

The six aptitudes are: design, story, symphony, empathy, play, and meaning. Mastering them is not sufficient, but leveraging these aptitudes has now become necessary for professional success and personal fulfillment in today's world. The introduction of the aptitudes that follow on the next page is written with multimedia-enhanced presentations in mind, but you could take the six aptitudes and apply them to the art of game design, programming, product design, project management, health care, teaching, retail, and so on. The slide below summarizes six of the key points found in Dan Pink's book. *(Original images in the slide are from a vector file from iStockphoto.com, file no. 700018.)*

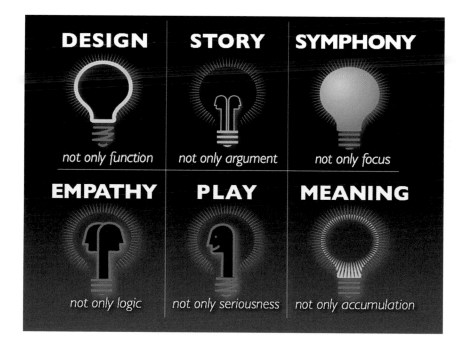

Design

To many business people, design is something you spread on the surface, like icing on a cake. It's nice, but not mission-critical. But this is not design to me, but rather "decoration." Decoration, for better or worse, is noticeable—sometimes enjoyable, sometimes irritating, but it is unmistakably there. However, the best designs are so well done that "the design" is never even noticed consciously by the observer/user, such as the design of a book or signage in an airport. (For example, we take conscious note of the messages which the design helped make utterly clear, but not the color palette, typography, concept, etc.)

Design starts at the beginning, not at the end; it's not an afterthought. If you use slideware in your presentation, the design of those visuals begins in the preparation stage before you have even turned on your computer. During the preparation stage, you slow down and "stop your busy mind" so that you may consider your topic and your objectives, your key messages, and your audience. Only then will you begin to sketch out ideas that will appear in some digital visual form later.

Story

Facts, information, data. Most of it is available online or can be sent to people in an email, a PDF attachment, or a hard copy through snail mail. Data and "the facts" have never been more widely available. Cognitive scientist Mark Turner calls storytelling "narrative imagining," something that is a key instrument of thought. We are wired to tell and receive stories. We are all born storytellers (and "storylisteners"). As kids we looked forward to "show and tell," and we gathered with our friends at recess and at lunchtime and told stories about real things and real events that mattered, at least they mattered to us.

But somewhere along the line, "story" became synonymous with fiction or even falsehood. So story and storytelling have been marginalized in business and academia as something serious people do not engage in. But gathering from what college students tell me, the best and most effective professors are the ones who tell true stories. My students tell me that the best professors (from their point of view) don't just go through the material in a book, but put their own personality, character, and experiences into the material in the form of a narrative, which is illuminating, engaging, and memorable. Stories can be used for good: for teaching, for sharing, for illuminating, and of course, for honest persuasion.

Symphony

Focus, specialization, and analysis have been important in the "information age," but in the "conceptual age," synthesis and the ability to use seemingly unrelated pieces to form and articulate the big picture before us is crucial, even a differentiator. Pink calls this aptitude "symphony."

The best presenters can illuminate the relationships that we may not have seen before. They can "see the relationships between relationships." Symphony requires that we become better at seeing—truly seeing in a new way. Anyone can deliver chunks of information and repeat findings represented visually in bullet points on a screen, but what's needed are those who can recognize the patterns, and who are skilled at seeing nuances and the simplicity that may exist in a complex problem. Symphony in the world of presentation does not mean "dumbing down" information into sound bytes and talking points so popular in the mass media, for example. Symphony is about utilizing our whole mind—logic, analysis, synthesis, intuition—to make sense of our world (i.e., our topic), find the big picture, and determine what is important and what is not before the day of our talk. It's also about deciding what matters and letting go of the rest.

Empathy

Empathy is emotional. It's about putting yourself in the position of others. It involves an understanding of the importance of the nonverbal cues of others and being aware of your own. Good designers, for example, have the ability to put themselves in the position of the user, the customer, or the audience member. This is a talent, perhaps, more than it's a skill that can be taught, but everyone can get better at this. Empathy allows a presenter, even without thinking about it, to notice when the audience is "getting it" and when they are not. The empathetic presenter can make adjustments based on his reading of this particular audience.

Play

In the conceptual age, says Pink, work is not just about seriousness but about play as well. Each presentation situation is different, but in many public speaking situations playfulness and humor can go a long way toward making a presentation palatable. "Humor" does not imply "jokiness" or clown-like informality, but rather good, old-fashioned humor that leads to laughter. Indian physician Madan Kataria points out in Pink's book that many people think that serious people are the best suited for business, that serious people are more responsible. "[But] that's not true," says Kataria. "That's yesterday's news. Laughing people are more creative people. They are more productive people." Somewhere along the line, we were sold the idea that a real business presentation must necessarily be dull, devoid of humor, and something to be endured, not enjoyed. And if you use slides—and God help you if you don't— the more complex, detailed, and ugly the better. This approach is still alive and well today, but we can hope in the future that this too will become "yesterday's news."

Satirist Tom Rielly gets playful in his 2007 TED presentation. TED/ leslieimage.com

Meaning

I don't want to put too fine a point on this, but making a presentation is an opportunity to make a small difference in the world (or your community, or your company, or school, etc.). A presentation that goes badly can have a devastating impact on your spirit and on your career. But a presentation that goes well can be extremely fulfilling for both you and the audience, and it might even help your career. Some say that we "are born for meaning" and live for self-expression and an opportunity to share that which we feel is important. If you are lucky, you're in a job that you feel passionate about. If so, then it's with excitement that you look forward to the possibility of sharing your expertise—your story—with others. Few things can be more rewarding than connecting with someone by teaching something new, or sharing that which you feel is very important with others.

Audiences are so used to death-by-PowerPoint that they've seemingly learned to see it as normal, even if not ideal. However, if you are different—if you exceed expectations and show them that you've thought about them, done your homework and know your material, and demonstrated through your actions how much you appreciate being there and that you are there for them—chances are you'll make an impact and a difference, even if it's just in the smallest of ways. There can be great meaning in even these small connections.

Design. Story. Symphony. Empathy. Play. Meaning. Dan Pink's *A Whole New Mind* gives us the context of the new world we're living in and why "high touch" talents—and that includes exceptional presentation skills—are so important today. Professionals today around the globe need to understand how and why the so-called right-brain aptitudes of design, story, symphony, empathy, play, and meaning are more important than ever. The best presentations of our generation will be created by professionals—engineers as well as CEOs and "creatives"—who have strong "whole mind" aptitudes and talents. These are not the only aptitudes needed by the modern presenter, but mastering these talents along with other important abilities such as strong analytical skills will take you far as a communicator in the "conceptual age."

Seth Godin

Speaker, blogger, author of *Meatball Sundae*
www.sethgodin.com

*Marketing guru and presenter extraordinaire Seth Godin
says presentation is about the transfer of emotion.*

It doesn't matter whether you're trying to champion at a church or a school or a Fortune 100 company, you're probably going to use PowerPoint. PowerPoint was developed by engineers as a tool to help them communicate with the marketing department—and vice versa. It's a remarkable tool because it allows very dense verbal communication. Yes, you could send a memo, but no one reads anymore. As our companies are getting faster and faster, we need a way to communicate ideas from one group to another. Enter PowerPoint.

PowerPoint could be the most powerful tool on your computer. But it's not. Countless innovations fail because their champions use PowerPoint the way Microsoft wants them to, instead of the right way.

Communication is about getting others to adopt your point of view, to help them understand why you're excited (or sad, or optimistic or whatever else you are.) If all you want to do is create a file of facts and figures, then cancel the meeting and send in a report.

Our brains have two sides. The right side is emotional, musical and moody. The left side is focused on dexterity, facts and hard data. When you show up to give a presentation, people want to use both parts of their brain. So they use the right side to judge the way you talk, the way you dress and your body language. Often, people come to a conclusion about your presentation by the time you're on the second slide. After that, it's often too late for your bullet points to do you much good. You can wreck a communication process with lousy logic or unsupported facts, but you can't complete it without emotion. Logic is not enough. Communication is the transfer of emotion.

Champions must sell—to internal audiences and to the outside world. If everyone in the room agreed with you, you wouldn't need to do a presentation, would you? You could save a lot of time by printing out a one-page project report and delivering it to each person. No, the reason we do presentations is to make a point, to sell one or more ideas.

If you believe in your idea, sell it. Make your point as hard as you can and get what you came for. Your audience will thank you for it, because deep down, we all want to be sold.

How to improve immediately

First, make slides that reinforce your words, not repeat them. Create slides that demonstrate, with emotional proof, that what you're saying is true not just accurate. No more than six words on a slide. EVER. There is no presentation so complex that this rule needs to be broken.

Second, don't use cheesy images. Use professional stock photo images. Talking about pollution in Houston? Instead of giving me four bullet points of EPA data, why not read me the stats but show me a photo of a bunch of dead birds, some smog and even a diseased lung? This is cheating! It's unfair! It works.

Third, no dissolves, spins or other transitions. Keep it simple.

Fourth, create a written document. A leave-behind. Put in as many footnotes or details as you like. Then, when you start your presentation, tell the audience that you're going to give them all the details of your presentation after it's over, and they don't have to write down everything you say. Remember, the presentation is to make an emotional sale. The document is the proof that helps the intellectuals in your audience accept the idea that you've sold them on emotionally. Don't hand out printouts of your slides. They don't work without you there.

The home run is easy to describe: You put up a slide. It triggers an emotional reaction in the audience. They sit up and want to know what you're going to say that fits in with that image. Then, if you do it right, every time they think of what you said, they'll see the image (and vice versa). Sure, this is different from the way everyone else does it. But everyone else is busy defending the status quo (which is easy) and you're busy championing brave new innovations, which is difficult.

Lyza Danger Gardner

Sample Slides

Here are a few sample slides from one of Seth's presentations. Without Seth, these visuals are almost meaningless. But with Seth's engaging narrative, the visuals help illuminate a memorable story.

A New Era Requires New Thinking

The skills necessary to be an effective communicator today are different than in the past. Today, literacy is not only about reading and writing text (though that is just as necessary), but also about understanding visual communication. Today, we need a higher degree of visual literacy and an understanding of the great power that imagery has for conveying important messages.

People who design visuals and use them in a live presentation typically regard PowerPoint as a kind of document-creation tool. Their principles and techniques seem to be largely influenced by conventional wisdom regarding the proper creation of business documents, such as letters, reports, spreadsheets, and so on. Many business people and students approach multimedia slides as if they were nothing more than glorified overhead transparencies that contain boxes for text, bullets, and some clip art.

If you want to learn how to become a better presenter, then look beyond the advice given in books about how to use PowerPoint or books on presentation skills (including this one). These books have their place, but you should be looking to other forms of proven, visual storytelling as well. Documentary films, for example, are a medium that tells a non-fiction story incorporating narration, interviews, audio, powerful video and still images, and at times, on-screen text. These are elements that can be incorporated into a live oral presentation as well. Cinema and presentations are different, but not as different as you may think. I have learned much about the use of imagery in storytelling from watching virtually every Ken Burns documentary ever produced.

The art of comics is another place to look for knowledge and inspiration. Comics, for example, are amazingly effective at partnering text and images that together form a powerful narrative which is engaging and memorable.

Comics and film are the two major ways that stories are told through imagery. A key point to remember is that the principles and techniques for creating a presentation for a conference or a keynote address have more in common with the principles and techniques behind the creation of a good documentary film or a good comic book than the creation of a conventional static business document with bullet points.

Letting Go

Part of the Presentation Zen approach to presenting well is learning to give up what we've learned about making presentations in the era of the PowerPoint deck and the cookie-cutter method of design and delivery. The first step is to stop letting our history and conditioning about what we "know" (or thought we knew) inhibit our being open to other ways of presentation. Seven sentences per slide? Some clip art thrown in for good measure? No one ever got fired for that, right? But if we remain attached to our past, we cannot learn anything new. We must open our minds so that we can see the world for what it is with a fresh new perspective.

The art of letting go of the past

EXERCISE

Either alone or with your work group or team, have a brainstorming session where you examine your current views and guidelines (if you have them) concerning your organization's presentations. How are your current presentations out of kilter? In what ways are they in sync? What questions should you be asking about presentation design and delivery that you have not asked in the past? What aspects of the design and delivery process have caused "suffering" for your presenters and your audiences? Have past efforts been focused too much on the comparatively inconsequential things? What are the "inconsequential" aspects and where can the focus shift?

In Sum

- Like a Japanese bento, great slide presentations contain appropriate content arranged in the most efficient, graceful manner without superfluous decoration. The presentation of the content is simple, balanced, and beautiful.

- Presentation Zen is an approach, not an inflexible list of rules to be followed by all the same way. There are many paths to designing and delivering presentations.

- The "Death by PowerPoint" approach is common and "normal" but it is not effective. The problem is not one of tools or technique so much as it is a problem of bad habits. Though some tools are better than others, it is possible to present effectively even with older versions of PowerPoint (or Keynote, etc.).

- In the "conceptual age" solid presentation skills are more important now than ever before. Presenting well is a "whole minded" skill. Good presenters target people's "left brain" and "right brain."

- Live talks enhanced by multimedia are about storytelling and have more in common with the art of documentary film than the reading of a paper document. Live talks today must tell a story enhanced by imagery and other forms of appropriate multimedia.

- We've learned some ineffective habits over the years. The first step to change is letting go of the past.

preparation

Such power there is in clear-eyed self-restraint.

— James Russell

2

Creativity, Limitations, and Constraints

In Chapter 3, we'll look at the first steps in the preparation stage, but first let's take a step back and look at something we usually do not think about when preparing a presentation: creativity. You may not think of yourself as being creative, let alone one of the creative professionals such as designers, writers, artists, and so on. But developing presentation content—especially content to be delivered with the aid of multimedia—is a creative act.

Recently, I gave a talk to college students where I encouraged them— begged them—to remember that they were, in fact, creative beings (they're human aren't they?). When I asked for a show of hands, most said they were not particularly creative. After all, they said, they were not designers or artists; they were business students. Then I asked them if they thought creating and delivering a business or conference presentation was a creative endeavor or something requiring a creative process. Only a few felt that it was. How about "design thinking?" Even fewer students understood how that related to a typical business presentation. "Design as differentiator?" Sure, students got that. But what, they said, did that have to do with presentations? Design was about iPods, and espresso machines, and sports cars, they said, but not about presentations and certainly "not PowerPoint."

Creating presentations is a supremely creative process. At least it should be. It's as much "right brain" as it is "left brain," and design does matter. Who said that business and creativity were mutually exclusive? Is business only about managing numbers and administration? Can't students become better business leaders tomorrow by learning how to become better design thinkers today? Aren't "design thinking" or "design mindfulness" and "creative thinking"

valuable aptitudes for all professionals, regardless of their discipline or their particular task at hand?

Once you realize that the preparation of a presentation is an act requiring creativity, not merely the assembling of facts and data in a linear fashion, you'll see that preparing a presentation is a "whole-minded" activity that requires as much right-brain thinking as it does left-brain thinking. In fact, while your research and background work may have required much logical analysis, calculation, and careful evidence gathering or so-called left-brain thinking, the transformation of your content into presentation form will require that you exercise much more of your so-called right brain.

Start With the Beginner's Mind

Zen teachings often speak of the "beginner's mind" or "child's mind." Like a child, one who approaches life with a beginner's mind is fresh, enthusiastic, and open to the vast possibilities of ideas and solutions before them. A child does not know what is not possible and so is open to exploration, discovery, and experimentation. If you approach creative tasks with the beginner's mind, you can see things more clearly as they are, unburdened by your fixed view, habits, or what conventional wisdom says it is (or should be). One who possesses a beginner's mind is not burdened by old habits or obsessed about "the way things are done around here" or with the way things could have or should have been done. A beginner is open and receptive and is more inclined to say "why not?" or "let's give it a shot," rather than "it's never been done" or "that's not common."

When you approach a new challenge as a true beginner (even if you are a seasoned adult), you need not be saddled with fear of failure or of making mistakes. If you approach problems with the "expert's mind," you are often blind to the possibilities. Your expert's mind is bound by the past and is not interested in the new and different and un-tried. Your expert's mind will say it can't be done (or shouldn't be done). Your beginner's mind will say, "I wonder if this can be done?"

If you approach a task with the beginner's mind, you are not afraid of being wrong. The fear of making a mistake, of risking an error, or of being told you are wrong is constantly with us. And that's a shame. Making mistakes is not the same thing as being creative, but if you are not willing to make mistakes, then it is impossible to be truly creative. If your state of mind is coming from a place of fear and risk avoidance, then you will always settle for the safe solutions—the solutions already applied many times before. Sometimes, the "path already taken" is the best solution. But you should not follow the path automatically without first seeing it for what it really is. When you are open to possibilities, you may find that the common way is the best way for your particular case. However, this will be a choice you made not by habit, but by reflection and in the spirit of a fresh beginner with fresh eyes and a new perspective.

Children are naturally creative, playful, and experimental. If you ask me, we were the most human when we were young kids. We "worked" on our art, sometimes for hours at a time without a break, because it was in us, though we didn't intellectualize it. As we got older, fears crept in, and doubts, and self-censoring, and over-thinking. The creative spirit is in us now; it's who we are. We just need to look at the kids around us to be reminded of that. And whether you are 28 or 88 today, it's never too late, because the child is still in you.

"In the beginner's mind there are many possibilities, in the expert's mind there are few."

—*Shunryu Suzuki*

You Are Creative

Creative power or creative imagination is not only for "the artists of the world," the painters, the sculptors, and so on—teachers also need the power of creativity. So do programmers, engineers, scientists, etc. You can see the application of creative genius in many professional fields. Remember, for example, that it was a group of brilliant and geeky-to-the-core, left-brain NASA engineers on the ground who in 1970 was able to jury-rig a solution to the life-threatening buildup of carbon dioxide in the damaged Apollo 13 spacecraft. Their heroic fix—literally involving duct tape and spare parts—was ingenious improvisation, it was imaginative, and it was creative.

Being creative does not mean wearing black turtlenecks and hanging out in jazz cafes sipping cappuccinos—it means using your whole mind to find solutions. Creativity means not being paralyzed by your methods and knowledge, but being able to think outside the box (sometimes very quickly) to find solutions to unforeseen problems. This kind of situation requires logic and analysis, but also big-picture thinking. And big-picture thinking is a right-brain, creative aptitude.

Back down here on earth, the seemingly mundane business of a conference presentation, designed and delivered with the help of slideware, can be a very creative thing. A presentation is an opportunity to differentiate yourself, or your organization, or your cause. It's your chance to tell the story of why your content is important and why it matters. It can be an opportunity to make a difference. So why look or talk like everyone else? Why strive to meet expectations? Why not surpass expectations and surprise people?

You are a creative person, probably far more creative than you think. All people should work toward tapping into their creative abilities and unleashing their imaginations.

If You Want to Write by Brenda Ueland (Graywolf Press) is one of the most inspiring and useful books I have ever read. The book was first published in 1938 and probably should have been titled "If You Want to Be Creative." The simple yet sage advice will be of interest not only to writers but also to anyone who yearns to be more creative in their work or to help others get in touch with their creative souls (this goes for programmers and epidemiologists, as well as designers and artists). This book should be required reading for all professionals or people aspiring to teach anyone about anything. Below are ideas inspired by Brenda Ueland that you should keep in mind when approaching the preparation of a presentation or any other creative endeavor in your work.

The Big Lie

Ah, the big lie we tell ourselves: "I am not creative." Sure, you might not be the next Picasso in your field (then again, who knows?). But it doesn't matter. What matters is to not close yourself down too early in the process of exploration. Failing is fine, necessary in fact. But avoiding experimentation or risk—especially out of fear of what others may think—is something that will gnaw at your gut more than any ephemeral failure. A failure is in the past. It's done and over. In fact, it doesn't exist. But worrying about "what might be if..." or "what might have been if I had..." are pieces of baggage you carry around daily. They're heavy, and they'll kill your creative spirit. Take chances and stretch yourself. You're only here on this planet once, and for a very short time at that. Why not just see how gifted you are? You may surprise someone. Most importantly, you may surprise yourself.

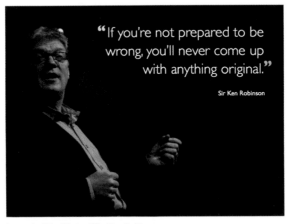

Image in this slide is of Sir Ken Robinson presenting at TED in 2006. Original photo courtesy of TED/ leslieimage.com.

Be a Pirate!

Inspiration. Where can you find it? A million places and in a million ways, but probably not by doing the same old routine, or by gossiping with staff in the break room about things that don't really matter. Sometimes, you can find inspiration in teaching. When you teach someone something important to you, you are reminded of why it matters, and the enthusiasm of the student—child or adult—is infectious and can energize you. Ueland says: "I helped them by trying to make them feel freer, bolder. Let her go! Be careless, reckless! Be a lion. Be a pirate!" You know it's important to be free, free like children are. You just need reminding occasionally.

Do Not Force It

Idling or doing nothing is important. Most of us, myself included, are obsessed with getting things done. We're afraid to be unproductive. And yet, the big ideas often come to you during your periods of "laziness," during those episodes of "wasting time." People need more time away from the direct challenges of work. Long walks on the beach, a jog through the forest, a bike ride, spending four to five hours in a coffee shop with the Sunday paper. During these times, your creative spirit is energized. Sometimes you need solitude and a break for slowing down so that you may see things differently. Managers who understand this and give their staff the time they need (which they can only do by genuinely trusting them) are the secure managers, and the best managers.

Enthusiasm

Put your love, passion, imagination, and spirit behind it. Without enthusiasm, there is no creativity. It may be a quiet enthusiasm, or it may be loud. It doesn't matter, so long as it is real. I remember once a guy commenting on a successful long-term project I did. He said to me, "Well, you have enthusiasm, I'll give you that..." It was a backhanded compliment. These are the people who get us down. Life is short. Don't hang out with people who dismiss the idea of enthusiasm, or worse still, with those who try to kill yours. Trying to impress others or worrying about what others may think of your enthusiasm or passion should be the last thing on your mind.

When forced to work within a strict framework the imagination is taxed to its utmost—and will produce its richest ideas. Given total freedom the work is likely to sprawl.

—T.S. Eliot

The Art of Working With Restrictions

My friends at Universal Studios Japan—Jasper von Meerheimb, Senior Art Director, and Sachiko Kawamura, Senior Environmental Graphic Designer— gave an excellent presentation recently for Design Matters Japan on the issue of how restrictive conditions put on creative projects can lead to inventive solutions. In their presentation, they talked about how to develop concepts and implement them under such constraints as limited time, space, and budget. For professional designers, creating great work under a thousand constraints and limitations imposed from the outside is simply the way the world of design works. Whether constraints are good or bad, enabling or crippling, is in a sense irrelevant; constraints are simply the way of the world. Still, as John Maeda points out in *The Laws of Simplicity* (MIT Press) "In the field of design there is the belief that with more constraints, better solutions are revealed." Time, for example, and the sense of urgency that it brings, is almost always a constraint, yet "urgency and the creative spirit go hand in hand…," Maeda says.

Using creativity and skill to solve a problem or design a message among a plethora of restrictions from the client, from the boss, and so on, is old hat to designers. They live it. Daily. However, for the millions of nondesigners with access to powerful design tools, the power and importance of constraints and limitations is not well understood. For those not trained in design, the task of creating presentation visuals (or posters, Web sites, newsletters, etc.) with today's software tools can make one either frustrated by the abundance of options or giddy in anticipation of applying their artistic sensibilities to decorate their work with an ever-increasing array of color, shapes, and special effects. Either condition can lead to designs and messages that suffer. What you can learn from professional designers is that (1) constraints and limitations are a powerful ally, not an enemy, and (2) creating your own self-imposed constraints, limitations, and parameters is often fundamental to good, creative work.

Self-imposed constraints can help you formulate clearer messages, including visual messages. In the various Zen arts, for example, you'll find that careful

Pecha-kucha: A Sign of the Changing Times

Pecha-kucha is a global presentation phenomenon started in 2003 by two Tokyo-based expatriate architects Mark Dytham and Astrid Klein. (*Pecha kucha* is Japanese for chatter.) Pecha-kucha is an example of the changing attitudes toward presentation and a wonderfully creative and un-conventional way "to do PowerPoint." The pecha-kucha method of presentation design and delivery is very simple. You must use 20 slides, each shown for 20 seconds, as you tell your story in sync with the visuals. That's 6 minutes and 40 seconds. Slides advance automatically and when you're done you're done. That's it. Sit down. The objective of these simple but tight restraints is to keep the presentations brief and focused and to give more people a chance to present in a single night.

Pecha-kucha Nights are held in over 80 cities from Amsterdam and Auckland to Venice and Vienna. The pecha-kucha nights in Tokyo are held in a hip multimedia space and the atmosphere on the night I attended was a cross between a cool user group meeting and a popular night club.

If nothing else, the pecha-kucha method is good training and good practice. Everyone should try pecha-kucha; it's a good exercise for getting your story down even if you do not use the method exactly for your own live talk. It doesn't matter whether or not you can implement the pecha-kucha "20x20 6:40" method exactly in your own company or school, but the spirit behind it and the concept of "restrictions as liberators" can be applied to most any presentation situation.

The method makes going deep difficult. But if there is a good discussion after a pecha-kucha type of presentation then it may work well even inside an organization. I can imagine having college students give this kind of presentation about their research followed by deeper questioning and probing by the instructor and class. Which would be more difficult for a student and a better indication of their knowledge: a 45 minute recycled and typical PowerPoint presentation, or a tight 6:40 presentation followed by 30 minutes of probing questions and discussion? On the other hand, if you can't tell the essence of your story in less than seven minutes, then you probably shouldn't be presenting anyway.

Checkout the Pecha Kucha Web site to find a Pecha Kucha Night near you.

www.pecha-kucha.org

study, practice, and adherence to strict guidelines (or "constraints") serve to bring out the creative energy of the individual. For example, haiku has a long tradition and strict guidelines, yet with much practice one can create a message (in 17 syllables or less) that captures both the details and the essence of a moment. The form of haiku may have strict rules, but it is the rules that can help you express your own "haiku moments" with both subtlety and with depth. In *Wabi Sabi Simple* (Adams Media Corporation), author Richard Powell comments on wabi sabi, discipline, and simplicity as they relate to such arts as bonsai and haiku:

> *"Do only what is necessary to convey what is essential. [C]arefully eliminate elements that distract from the essential whole, elements that obstruct and obscure.... Clutter, bulk, and erudition confuse perception and stifle comprehension, whereas simplicity allows clear and direct attention."*
>
> -Richard Powell

Life is about living with limitations and constraints of one type or another, but constraints are not necessarily bad, in fact they are helpful, even inspiring as they challenge us to think differently and more creatively about a particular problem. While problems such as a sudden request to give a 20-minute sales pitch or a 45-minute overview of our research findings have built-in limitations—such as time, tools, and budget—we can increase our effectiveness by stepping back, thinking long and hard, and determining ways we can set our own parameters and constraints as we set out to prepare and design our next presentation with greater clarity, focus, balance, and purpose.

As daily life becomes even more complex, and the options and choices continue to mount, crafting messages and making designs that are clear, simple, and concise becomes all the more important. Clarity and simplicity— often this is all people want or need, yet it's increasingly rare (and all the more appreciated when it's discovered). You want to surprise people? You want to exceed their expectations? Then consider making it beautiful, simple, clear... and great. The "greatness" may just be found in what was left out, not in what was left in. It takes creativity and the courage to be different. Your audience is praying that you'll be both creative and courageous.

In Sum

- Preparing, designing, and delivering a presentation is a creative act, and you are a creative being.

- Creativity requires an open mind and a willingness to be wrong.

- Restrictions and limitations are not the enemy; they are a great ally.

- As you prepare a presentation, exercise restraint and keep these three words in mind always: simplicity, clarity, brevity.

3

Planning Analog

Once of the most important things you can do in the initial stage of preparing for your presentation is to get away from your computer. A fundamental mistake people make is spending almost the entire time thinking about their talk and preparing their content while sitting in front of a computer screen. Before you design your presentation, you need to see the big picture and identify your core messages— or the single core message. This can be difficult unless you create a stillness of mind for yourself, something which is hard to do while puttering around in slideware.

Right from the start, most people plan their presentations using software tools. In fact, the software makers encourage this, but I don't recommend it. There's just something about paper and pen and sketching out rough ideas in the "analog world" in the early stages that seems to lead to more clarity and better, more creative results when we finally get down to representing our ideas digitally. Since you will be making your presentation accompanied by PowerPoint or Keynote, you will be spending plenty of time in front of a computer later. I call preparing the presentation away from the computer "going analog," as opposed to "going digital" at the computer.

A Bike or a Car?

Software companies have oversold us on the idea of following templates and wizards, which while sometimes useful, often take us places we do not really want to go. In this sense, Edward Tufte is right when he says there is a cognitive style to PowerPoint that leads to an oversimplification of our content and obfuscation of our message. Slideware applications like PowerPoint and Keynote are wonderful for displaying media in support of our talk, but if we are not careful these applications also point us down a road that we may not have gone otherwise.

More than 20 years ago, Steve Jobs and others in Silicon Valley were talking about the great potential of personal computers and how these tools should be designed and used in a way that enhanced the great potential that exists within each of us. Here's what Steve Jobs said back then in a documentary called *Memory and Imagination* (Michael Lawrence Films):

> *"What a computer is to me is it's the most remarkable tool that we've ever come up with, and it's the equivalent of a bicycle for our minds."*
>
> — *Steve Jobs*

Humans, it seems, are not such an efficient animal when it comes to locomotion compared to other animals. But a human on a bicycle is the most efficient animal on the planet. The bicycle amplifies our input in an enormously productive way. Isn't this what a computer—the most magnificent tool of our time—should do?

During the planning stage of a presentation, does your computer function as a "bicycle for your mind," amplifying your own capabilities and ideas, or is it more like a "car for your mind" with prepackaged formulas that make your ideas soft? Your mind benefits when you use the computer like a bike but loses out when you rely only on your computer's power the way you rely on your car's power. It's important to understand principles of presentation creation, and design, not merely software application rules to be obediently followed or the tips and tricks of the day. The best software, in many cases, does not so much point the way as it gets out of the way, helping us to amplify our own ideas and abilities. One way to ensure that your computer and your software applications remain great tools of amplification for your ideas and your presentation is to first turn off the computer and walk away from it. You'll be back soon enough.

Paper, Whiteboards, or a Stick in the Sand

My favorite tools used in preparation for a presentation (or any other project for that matter) usually consist of a large pad of yellow legal paper and colored pens, a moleskin storyboard book, or if I am in my office, a large whiteboard. As wonderful as digital technology is, I don't think anything is as quick, easy, and immediate as a simple pad and pencil, and nothing gives me space to jot down ideas quite like a massive whiteboard.

Most business people and even college students do all the preparation of their presentations directly in slideware. In this regard, you can learn a lot from professional designers. Most professional designers—even young new media designers who've grown up on computers—usually do much of their planning and brainstorming on paper.

This became very clear to me one day at Apple when I visited a senior director for one of the creative teams on the other side of the Apple campus to get his input on the project we were working on. He said he had sketched out a lot of ideas that he wanted to show me. I assumed that he had prepared some slides or a movie or at least printed out some color images in Illustrator or Photoshop to show me. But when I arrived at his office, I found that the beautiful Apple Cinema Display on his desk was off (I learned later that this talented creative director worked for days without ever turning on his Mac), and he instead had sketched out his ideas on a scroll of white paper that stretched about five meters across his office wall. This large scroll was a combination of hand-drawn images and text resembling a large comic strip. The creative director started at one end of the "strip" and walked me through his ideas, stopping occasionally to add a word or a graphic element. After our meeting, he rolled up his sketches and said "take 'em with you." Later I would incorporate his ideas into our internal presentation in PowerPoint.

"If you have the ideas,
you can do a lot without machinery.
Once you have those ideas,
the machinery starts working for you….
Most ideas you can do pretty darn well
with a stick in the sand."

—*Alan Kay*
(Interview in Electronic Learning, April 1994)

Pen and Paper

I spend a lot of time working outside of my office in coffee shops, in parks, and while riding on the Japanese Bullet Train (Shinkansen) on one of my trips to Tokyo. And although I have a MacBook Pro or PC with me at virtually all times, it is pen and paper that I use to privately brainstorm, explore ideas, make lists, and generally sketch out my ideas. I could use the computer, but I find—as many do—that the act of holding a pen in my hand to sketch out ideas seems to have a greater, more natural connection to my right brain and allows for a more spontaneous flow and rhythm for visualizing and recording ideas. Compared to sitting at a keyboard, the act of using paper and pen to explore ideas, and the visualization of those ideas, seems far more powerful.

Whiteboards

I often use a large whiteboard in my office to sketch out my ideas. The whiteboard works for me because I feel uninhibited and free to brainstorm and sketch ideas on a bigger scale. I can also step back (literally) from what I have sketched out and imagine how it might flow logically when slides are added later. The advantage of a whiteboard (or chalkboard) is that you can use it with small groups to record concepts and direction. As I write down key points and assemble an outline and structure, I can draw quick ideas for visuals, such as charts or photos that will later appear in the slides. I draw sample images that I can use to support a particular point, say, a pie chart here, a photo there, perhaps a line graph in this section, and so on.

You may be thinking that this is a waste of time: why not just go into PowerPoint and create your images there so you do not have to do it twice? Well, the fact is, if I tried to create a storyboard first in PowerPoint, it would actually take longer, as I would constantly have to go from normal view to slide sorter view to see the whole picture. The analog approach (paper or whiteboard) to sketch out my ideas and create a rough storyboard really helps solidify and simplify my message in my own head. I then have a far easier time laying out those ideas in PowerPoint or Keynote. I usually do not even have to look at the whiteboard or legal pad when I am in slideware, because the analog process alone gave me a clear visual image of how I want the content to flow. I glance at my notes to remind me of what visuals I thought of using at certain points and then go to iStockphoto.com or to my own library of high-quality stock images to find the perfect image.

Post-its

Large sheets of paper and marking pens—as "old school" as they may seem—can be wonderful, simple tools for initially sketching out your ideas or recording the ideas of others. When I was at Apple, I sometimes led brainstorming sessions by sticking large Post-its on the wall. I wrote the ideas down or others stepped up to the front and sketched out their ideas "the old fashioned way" while arguing their point or elaborating on ideas by others. It was messy, but it was a good mess. By the end of the session, the walls were filled with large "Post-its," which I then took back to my office and stuck on my own walls. As I (and others) developed the structure and visuals for the future presentation, we often referred to the sheets on the walls, which were on display for days or weeks. Having the content on the walls made it easier to see the big picture. It also made it easier to see what items could be cut and which were clearly essential to the core message.

Though you may be using digital technology to create your visuals and display them when you deliver your presentation, the act of speaking and connecting to an audience—to persuade, sell, or inform—is very much analog. For this reason, it only seems natural to go analog while preparing and clarifying your presentation's content, purpose, and goals.

Slowing Down to See

Slowing down is not just good advice for a healthier, happier, more fulfilling life, but it is also a practice that leads to greater clarity. Your instinct may be to say that this is ridiculous, business is all about speed. First to innovate. First to market. First and fast.

What I am talking about here, however, is a state of mind. You have many things on your plate, no doubt. You are busy. But "busy" is not really the problem. Sure, there never seems to be enough time in the day to do things the way you would prefer to do them, and we all face time constraints. But time constraints can also be a be a great motivator, bringing a sense of urgency that stimulates creative thinking and the discovery of solutions to problems. The problem today, though, is not "busy" but "busyness."

Busyness is that uncomfortable feeling you have when you are feeling rushed, distracted, and a bit unfocused and preoccupied. Although you may be accomplishing tasks, you wished you could do better. You know you can. But in spite of your best intentions, you find it difficult to create a state of mind that is contemplative rather than reactionary. You try. You take a deep breath. You begin to think about the big presentation next week. So you open up your application and begin to think. Then the office phone rings, but you let it go to voice mail because your boss is calling you on your mobile phone at the same time. "Need TPS reports ASAP!" she says. Then your email application notifies you that you've got new messages, including one from your biggest client with the subject line "Urgent! TPS reports missing!!!" Then your co-worker pops his head in the door "Hey, did you hear about the missing TPS reports?" So you get to work reacting, even though you know that dealing with the reports could actually wait until another time. In this sort of environment, it is nearly impossible to slow down.

Busyness kills creativity. Busyness leads to the creation and display of a lot of PowerPoint decks that substitute for engaging, informative, or provocative meetings or seminars or keynote speeches where actual conversations could and should be taking place. But people feel rushed, even frantic. So they slap together some slides from past presentations and head to their presentation. Communication suffers… the audience suffers. Yes, we're all insanely busy, but this is just all the more reason why we owe it to ourselves and to our audience not to waste their time with perfunctory "slideshows from hell." To do something better takes a different mindset, and it takes time and space away from "busyness."

When you think about it, the really great creatives—designers, musicians, even entrepreneurs, programmers, etc.—are the ones who see things differently and who have unique insights, perspectives, and questions. (Answers are important, but first come questions.) This special insight and knowledge, as well as plain ol' gut feel and intuition, can only come about for many of us when slowing down, stopping, and seeing all sides of our particular issue. It does not matter if you are a scientist, engineer, medical doctor, or businessperson, when you prepare a presentation you are "a creative," and you need time away from the computer and dealing with digital outlines and slides. And whenever possible, you also need time alone.

One reason why many presentations are so ineffective is that people today just do not take—or do not have—enough time to step back and really assess what is important and what is not. They often fail to bring anything unique, creative, or new to the presentation, not because they are not smart or creative beings, but because they did not have the time alone to slow down and contemplate the problem. Seeing the big picture and finding your core message may take some time alone "off the grid." There are many ways to find solitude, and you don't even have to be alone. I find a very pleasant form of solitude, for example, at "my Starbucks" down the street from my apartment in central Osaka, where the friendly staff know me by name. It's a bustling café, but also cozy and relaxing with loads of overstuffed sofas and chairs and jazz playing softly in the background. And I am left alone.

I'm not suggesting that more time alone is a panacea for a lack of ideas or that it necessarily leads to more creativity or better solutions, but I think you will be pleasantly surprised if you can create more time every day, every week, month, and year to experience solitude. For me at least, solitude helps achieve greater focus and clarity, while also allowing me to see the big picture. Clarity and the big picture are the fundamental elements that are missing from most presentations.

I don't want to overly romanticize solitude. Too much "alonetime" obviously can be a bad thing as well, yet in today's busy world, too much solitude is a problem faced by few of us. For most professionals, finding some time alone can be a great struggle indeed.

The Need for Solitude

Many believe that solitude is a basic human need, and to deny it is unhealthy for both mind and body. Dr. Ester Buchholz, a psychoanalyst and clinical psychologist who passed away in 2004 at the age of 71, did quite a bit of research on solitude during her career, what she called "alonetime." Dr. Buchholz thought that society undervalued solitude and alone time and overvalued attachment. Dr. Buchholz thought that periods of solitude were important if we were to tap our creative potential. "Life's creative solutions require alonetime," she said. "Solitude is required for the unconscious to process and unravel problems." The second half of Dr. Buchholz's quote appears in the slide below, a slide I have used in some of my talks on creativity.

> **"**Others inspire us, information feeds us, practice improves our performance, but we need quiet time to figure things out, to emerge with new discoveries, to unearth original answers. **"**
>
> — Ester Buchholz

In order to be open to creativity, one must have the capacity for constructive use of solitude. One must overcome the fear of being alone.

—Rollo May

Asking the Right Questions

It is said that Buddha described the human condition as being much like that of a man who has been shot with an arrow. That is, the situation is both painful and urgent. But let's imagine that instead of asking for immediate medical assistance for his predicament, the man asks details about the bow that shot the arrow. He asks about the manufacturer of the arrow. He wonders about the background of the people who made the bow and arrow, how they arrived at the color choice, what kind of string they used, and so on. The man asks many inconsequential questions, overlooking the immediate problem.

Our lives are a bit like this. We often do not see the reality right in front of us, they say, because we chase ephemeral things, such as salary, the perfect job, a bigger house, more status, and we worry about losing what we have. The Buddhist would say that life is filled with "duhhka" (suffering, pain, loss, a feeling of dissatisfaction)—we need only to open our eyes to see this. In a similar way, the current state of business and academic presentations bring about a fair amount of "suffering" in the form of ineffectiveness, wasted time, and general dissatisfaction, both for the presenter and for the audience.

There is much discussion today among professionals on the issue of how to make presentations and presenters better. For businesses and presenters, the situation is both "painful and urgent" in a sense. It's important. Yet, much of the discussion focuses on software applications and techniques. What application should I get? Should I get a Mac or a PC? What animations and transitions are best? What is the best remote control? This talk is not completely inconsequential, but it often dominates discussions on presentation effectiveness. The focus on technique and software features often distracts us from what we should be examining. Many of us spend too much time fidgeting with and worrying about bullets and images on slides during the preparation stage instead of thinking about how to craft a story which is the most effective, memorable, and appropriate for our particular audience.

The Wrong Questions

In obsessing on technique and tricks and effects, we are a bit like the man who has an arrow stuck in him—our situation is urgent and painful, yet we are asking the wrong questions and focusing on that which is relatively inconsequential.

Two of the more inconsequential questions I get—and I get these a lot—are "How many bullets should I use per slide?" and "How many slides per presentation is good?" My answer? "It depends on a great many things... how about zero?" This gets people's attention, but it's not the most popular answer. I'll deal with the bullet points question in the chapter on slide design (Chapter 6). As for how many slides, that really is the wrong question. There are too many variables involved to make a concrete rule to be followed by all the same way. I have seen long, dull presentations from presenters who used only five slides, and content-rich, engaging presentations from presenters who used over 200 slides (and vise versa). The number of slides is not the point. If your presentation is successful, the audience will have no idea how many slides you used, nor will they care.

Questions We Should Be Asking

OK, so you're alone. You've got a pad and a pen. You're relaxed, and your mind is still. Now picture in your mind that presentation you get to give (notice I did not say have to give) next month... or next week, or (gulp) tomorrow. Jot down the answers to these questions:

- How much time do I have?
- What's the venue like?
- What time of the day?
- Who is the audience?
- What's their background?
- What do they expect of me (us)?
- Why was I asked to speak?
- What do I want them to do?
- What visual medium is most appropriate for this particular situation and audience?
- What is the fundamental purpose of my talk?
- What's the story here?
- And this is the most fundamental question of all. Stripped down to its essential core:

What is my absolutely central point?

Or put it this way: If the audience could remember only one thing (and you'll be lucky if they do), what do you want it to be?

Two Questions: What's Your Point? Why Does It Matter?

A lot of the presentations I attend feature a person from a specialized field giving a talk—usually with the help of PowerPoint—to an audience of business people who are not specialists in the presenter's technical field. This is a common presentation situation. For example, an expert in the area of, say, biofuel technology may be invited to give a presentation to a local chamber of commerce about the topic and about what their company does, what the average person can do, etc. Recently, I attended such an event, and after the hour-long talk was over I realized that the presentation was a miracle of sorts: until that day I didn't think it was possible to actually listen to someone make a presentation with slides in my native language of English and for me to genuinely not understand a single point that was made. Not one. Nada. I wanted my hour back.

The wasted hour was not the fault of PowerPoint or bad slides, however. The presentation would have been greatly improved if the presenter had simply kept two questions in mind in preparing for the talk: What's my point? And why does it matter?

It is hard enough for presenters to find their core message and express it in a way that is unambiguously understood. But why does it matter? This is where people really stumble. This is because the presenter is so close to his material that the question of why it should matter simply seems obvious, too obvious to make explicit. Yet, that is what people (including most audiences) are hoping and praying that you'll tell them. "Why should we care?" That's going to take persuasion, emotion, and empathy in addition to logical argument. Empathy in the sense that the presenter understands that not everyone will see what to him is obvious, or that others may understand well but not see why it should matter to them. When preparing material for a talk, good presenters try to put themselves in the shoes of their audience members.

Getting back to my wasted hour. The presenter, who was smart, accomplished, and professional, failed before he even started. The slides looked like they were the same ones used in previous presentations to more technical audiences inside his company, an indication that he had not thought first and foremost about his audience on that day. He failed to answer the important question: "Why does it matter?" He also failed in the preparation stage to remember that presentation opportunities like this one are about contributing something and leaving something important behind for the audience.

Dakara Nani? (So What?)

In Japanese I often say to myself, "dakara nani?" or "sore de...?" which translates roughly as "so what?!" or "your point being...?" I say this often while I am preparing my material or helping others prepare their talks. When building the content of your presentation, you should always put yourself in the shoes of the audience and ask "so what?" Really ask yourself the tough questions throughout the planning process. For example, is your point relevant? It may be cool, but is it important to further your story, or is it included only because it seems impressive to you (but few others)? Surely you have been in an audience and wondered how what the presenter was talking about was relevant or supported his core point. If you can't really answer that question, then cut that bit of content out of your talk.

Can You Pass the "Elevator Test?"

If "dakara nani" does not work for you, then check the clarity of your presentation's core message with the elevator test. This exercise forces you to "sell" your message in 30–45 seconds. Imagine this is the situation: You have been scheduled to pitch a new idea to the head of product marketing at your company, one of the leading technology manufactures in the world. Both schedules and budgets are tight; this is an extremely important opportunity for you if you are to succeed at getting the OK from the executive team. When you arrive at the admin desk outside the vice-president's office, suddenly she comes out with her coat and briefcase in hand and says, "...sorry, something's come up, give me your idea as we walk down to my car..." Imagine such a scenario. Could you sell your idea in the elevator ride and the walk to the parking lot? Sure, the scenario is unlikely, but possible. What is very possible, however, is for you to be asked without notice to shorten your talk down, from, say, 20 minutes, to five minutes (or from a scheduled one hour to 30 minutes). Could you do it? True, you may never have to, but practicing what you would do in such a case forces you to get your message down and make your overall content tighter and clearer.

Handouts Can Set You Free

If you create a proper handout as a leave-behind for your presentation during the preparation phase, then you will not feel compelled to say everything about your topic in your talk. Preparing a proper document—with as much detail as you think necessary—frees you to focus on what is most important for your particular audience on your particular day. If you write a proper document you will also not worry about the exclusion of charts or figures or related points to your topic. You can't say everything in your talk. Many presenters include everything under the sun in their slides "just in case" or to show that they are "serious people." It is common to create slides with lots of text and detailed charts, etc. because the slides will also serve as a leave-behind document. Big mistake (see sidebar on "slideumentation"). Instead, prepare a detailed document for a handout and keep the slides simple. And never distribute a printed version of your slides as a handout. Why? David S. Rose, expert presenter and one of New York City's most successful technology entrepreneurs put it to me this way:

> "Never, ever hand out copies of your slides, and certainly not before your presentation. That is the kiss of death. By definition, since slides are "speaker support" material, they are there in support of the speaker... YOU. As such, they should be completely incapable of standing by themselves, and are thus useless to give to your audience, where they will simply be guaranteed to be a distraction. The flip side of this is that if the slides can stand by themselves, why the heck are you up there in front of them?"

> —David S. Rose

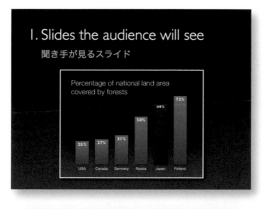

1. Slides the audience will see
聞き手が見るスライド

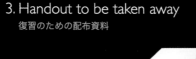

2. Notes only you will see
話し手が使うメモ

3. Handout to be taken away
復習のための配布資料

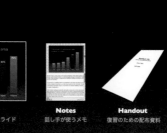

Three Parts of a Presentation

If you remember that there are three components to your presention—the slides, your notes, and the handout—then you will not feel the need to place so much information (text, data, etc.) in your slides. Instead, you can place that information in your notes (for the purpose of rehearsing or as a backup "just in case") or in the handout. This point has been made by presentation experts such as Cliff Atkinson, yet most people still fill their slides with reams of text and hard-to-see data and simply print out their slides instead of creating a document. (I have used the four slides on this page while making this point during my live talks on presentation design.)

Create a Document Not a Slideument

Slides are slides. Documents are documents.
They aren't the same thing. Attempts
to merge them result in what I call the
"slideument." The creation of the slideument
stems from a desire to save time. People
think they are being efficient and simplifying
things. A kind of kill-two-birds-with-one-
stone approach, or *iiseki ni cho* in Japanese.
Unfortunately (unless you're a bird), the only
thing "killed" is effective communication.
Intentions are good, but results are bad.
This attempt to save time by creating a
slideument reminds me of a more fitting
Japanese proverb: *nito o oumono wa itto mo ezu* or "chase two hares and get none."

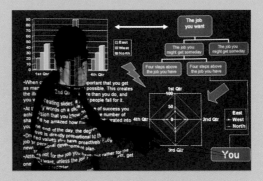

Projected slides should be as visual as possible and support your points quickly,
efficiently, and powerfully. The verbal content, the verbal proof, evidence, and
appeal/emotion come mostly from your spoken word. But your handouts (takeaway
documents) are completely different. You aren't there to supply the verbal content
and answer questions so you must write in a way that provides at least as much
depth and scope as your live presentation. Often, however, even more depth and
background information is appropriate since people can read much faster than you
can speak. Sometimes, the presentation is on material found in the speaker's book
or a long journal article. In that case, the handout can be quite concise; the book
or research paper is where people can go to learn more.

Do Conferences Encourage Slideumentation?

Proof that we live in a world dominated by "bad PowerPoint"—many conferences
today require speakers to follow uniform PowerPoint guidelines and submit their
PowerPoint files far in advance of the conference. The conference now takes
these "standardized PowerPoints" and prints them in a large conference binder
or includes them in the conference DVD for attendees to take home. What the
conference organizers are implying is that a cryptic series of slides featuring bullet
points and titles makes for both good visual support in your live presentation and
for credible documentation of your presentation content long after your talk has
ended. This forces the conference speaker into a catch-22 situation. The presenter
must say to herself: "Do I design visuals that clearly support my live talk or do I
create slides that more resemble a document to be read later?" Most presenters

compromise and shoot for the middle, resulting in poor supporting visuals for the live talk and a series of document-like slides filled with text and other data that do not read well (and are therefore not read). These pseudo-documents do not read well because a series of small boxes with text and images on sheets of paper do not a document make.

The slideument isn't effective, and it isn't efficient, and it isn't pretty. Attempting to have slides serve both as projected visuals and as stand-alone handouts makes for bad visuals and bad documentation. Yet, this is a typical, acceptable approach. PowerPoint (or Keynote) is a tool for displaying visual information, information that helps you tell your story, make your case, prove your point, and engage your audience. PowerPoint and Keynote are not good tools, however, for making written documents—that's what word processors are for.

Why don't conference organizers request that speakers instead send a written document (with a specified maximum page length) that covers the main points of their presentation with appropriate detail and depth? A Word or PDF document that is written in a concise and readable fashion with a bibliography and links to even more detail, for those who are interested, would be far more effective. When I get back home from the conference, do organizers really think I'm going to attempt to read pages full of PowerPoint slides? One does not read a printout of someone's two-
month old PowerPoint deck, one guesses, decodes, and attempts to glean meaning from the series of low-resolution titles, bullets, charts, and clip art. At least they do that for a while… until they give up. With a written document, however, there is no reason for shallowness or ambiguity (assuming one writes well).

To be different and effective, use a well-written, detailed document for your handout and well-designed, simple, intelligent graphics for your visuals. Now that would be atypical. And while it may be more effort on your part, the quality of your visuals and takeaway documents will be dramatically improved. This may not be the easiest solution, but it seems quite simple, straightforward, and clear. It is the simplest.

Avoiding the Slideument

The slide on the left displays obesity rates for 30 countries in two formats. The table and bar graph were made in Excel and pasted into PowerPoint. It is common for people to take detailed data like this from Excel and Word documents used in reports and paste them into display slides for a presentation. But it's rarely necessary to include all the data in an on-screen visual for a short live talk. If it is necessary to examine so much data during the talk, then place the table and charts in a paper and hand it out during your talk. (The low resolution and limited real-estate of display screens makes it difficult to read labels at such small sizes anyway.) It is usually better to use just the parts of the data that truthfully and accurately support your point. In this example the point is to show how the US rate is much higher than the rate in Japan. It is not necessary to show the rates for so many other countries. The obesity rates for the other countries can be included in the takeaway handout.

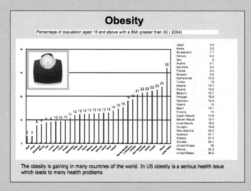

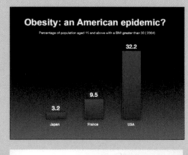

Instead of using a detailed chart which will appear cluttered and difficult to read, try creating a simpler visual for the slide and place the detailed charts and tables in the takeaway document where you have more space to present the details in a proper layout.

The Benefit of Planning Well

If you prepare well, and really get your story down pat—down well enough to pass the elevator test—then you really can tell your core message well in any situation. A friend of mine, Jim in Singapore, sent me an email recently sharing a good example of what can happen when you really get your story down in the preparation stage.

> *Dear Garr... got this new prospect and have been trying to get in front of the guy for months. Finally get the word he'll see me next week. I know he is a super short attention span guy so I used a simple approach and agonized over the content and the key message and then the graphics. We get to the office and begin with the usual small talk that starts a meeting and suddenly I realize we've gone over the points of the presentation in our conversation and he has agreed to move forward. Then he looks at his watch and says great to see you thanks for coming in. As we walk out of the building the two guys that work for me say hey you never even pulled out the presentation and he still bought the deal—that was great!*
>
> *Meanwhile I'm in a complete funk: "What about all my preparation time? He never even saw my presentation. What a waste of time putting the whole thing together!" Then the light went on. Presentation preparation is about organizing thoughts and focusing the storytelling so it's all clear to your audience. I was able to articulate the points because I had worked those through in the preparation of the presentation. Even the graphics had made me think the presentation through and became a part of the presentation even though the audience never saw them.*

This is an excellent point Jim makes here. If you prepare well, the preparation process *itself* should help you really know your story. With proper preparation, you should be able to still tell your story if the projector breaks five minutes before the presentation or if the client says "to heck with the slides, just give it to me straight."

The planning stage should be the time when your minds are clearest and all barriers removed. I love technology, and I think slideware can be very effective in many situations. But for planning, go analog—paper and pen, whiteboards, a notepad in your pocket as you take a walk down the beach with your dog... whatever works for you. Peter Drucker said it best: "The computer is a moron." You and your ideas (and your audience) are all that matter. So try getting away from the computer in the early stages, the time when your creativity is needed most. For me at least, clarity of thinking and a generation of ideas come when my computer and I are far apart.

The purpose behind getting off the grid, slowing down, and using paper or whiteboards, etc. during the preparation stage is to better identify, clarify, and crystallize your core message. The core is what it is all about. Again, if your audience remembers only one thing, what should that be? And why? By getting your ideas down and key message absolutely clear in your mind and visualized on paper first, you'll be able to organize and design slides and other multimedia that support and magnify your important content.

In Sum

- Slow down your busy mind to see your problem and goals more clearly.

- Find time alone to see the big picture.

- For greater focus, try turning off the computer and going analog.

- Use paper and pens or a whiteboard first to record and sketch out your ideas.

- Key questions: What's your main (core) point? Why does it matter?

- If your audience remembers only one thing, what should it be?

- Preparing a detailed handout keeps you from feeling compelled to cram everything into your visuals.

Crafting the Story

During your time off the grid, you brainstormed alone or perhaps with a small group of people. You stepped back to get the big picture, and you identified your core message. You now have a clearer picture of the presentation content and focus, even if you do not have all the details worked out yet. The next step is to give your core message and supporting messages a logical structure. Structure will help bring order to your presentation and make it easier for you to deliver it smoothly, and for your audience to understand your message easily.

Before you go from analog to digital—taking your ideas from sketches on paper and laying them out in PowerPoint or Keynote—it is important to keep in mind what makes your ideas resonate with people. What makes some presentations absolutely brilliant and others forgettable? If your goal is to create a presentation that is memorable, then you need to consider at all times how you can craft messages that stick.

What Makes Messages Stick?

Most of the great books that will help you make better presentations are not specifically about presentations at all, and certainly not about how to use slideware. One such book is *Made to Stick* (Random House) by Chip Heath and Dan Heath. The Heath brothers were interested in what makes some ideas effective and memorable and other ideas utterly forgettable. Some stick and others fade away. Why? What the authors found—and explain simply and brilliantly in their book—is that "sticky" ideas have six key principles in common: simplicity, unexpectedness, concreteness, credibility, emotions, and stories. And yes, these six compress nicely into the acronym SUCCESs.

The six principles are relatively easy to incorporate into messages—including presentations and keynote addresses—but most people fail to use them. Why? The authors say that the biggest reason why most people fail to craft effective or "sticky" messages is because of what they call the "Curse of Knowledge." The Curse of Knowledge is essentially the condition whereby the deliverer of the message cannot imagine what it's like not to possess his level of background knowledge on the topic. When he speaks in abstractions to the audience, it makes perfect sense to him, but to him alone. In his mind it seems simple and obvious. The six principles—SUCCESs—are your weapons, then, to fight your own Curse of Knowledge (we all have it) to make messages that stick.

Here's an example that the authors used early in their book to explain the difference between a good, sticky message and a weak yet garden-variety message. Look at these two messages which address the same idea. One of them should seem very familiar to you.

> *"Our mission is to become the international leader in the space industry through maximum team-centered innovation and strategically targeted aerospace initiatives."*

Or

> *"...put a man on the moon and return him safely by the end of the decade."*

The first message sounds similar to CEO-speak today and is barely comprehensible, let alone memorable. The second message—which is actually from a 1961 speech by John F. Kennedy—has every element of SUCCESs, and it motivated a nation toward a specific goal that changed the world. JFK, or at least his speechwriters, knew that abstractions are not memorable, nor do they motivate. Yet how many speeches today by CEOs and other leaders contain phrases like "maximize shareholder value yada, yada, yada?" Here's a quick summary of the six principles from *Made to Stick* that you should keep in mind when crystallizing your ideas and crafting your messages for speeches, presentations, or any other form of communication.

- **Simplicity.** If everything is important, then nothing is important. If everything is a priority, then nothing is a priority. You must be ruthless in your efforts to simplify—not dumb down—your message to its absolute core. We're not talking about stupid sound bites here. Every idea can be reduced to its bare essential meaning, if you work hard enough. For your presentation, what's the key point? What's the core? Why does (or should) it matter?

- **Unexpectedness.** You can get people's interest by violating their expectations. Surprise people. Surprise will get their interest. But to sustain their interest, you have to stimulate their curiosity. The best way to do that is to pose questions or open holes in people's knowledge and then fill those holes. Make the audience aware that they have a gap in their knowledge and then fill that gap with the answers to the puzzle (or guide them to the answers). Take people on a journey.

- **Concreteness.** Use natural speech and give real examples with real things, not abstractions. Speak of concrete images, not of vague notions. Proverbs are good, say the Heath brothers, at reducing abstract concepts to concrete, simple, but powerful (and memorable) language. For example, the expression "*iiseki ni cho*" or "kill two birds with one stone"? It's easier than saying something like "let's work toward maximizing our productivity by increasing efficiency across many departments, etc." And the phrase "…go to the moon and back" by JFK (and Ralph Kramden before him)? Now that's concrete. You can visualize that.

- **Credibility.** If you are famous in your field, you may have built-in credibility (but even that does not go as far as it used to). Most of us, however, do not have that kind of credibility, so we reach for numbers and cold hard data to support our claims as market leaders and so on. Statistics, say the Heath brothers, are not inherently helpful. What's important is the context and the meaning. Put it in terms that people can visualize. "Five hours of battery life" or "Enough battery life to watch your favorite TV shows nonstop on your iPod during your next flight from San Francisco to New York"? There are many ways to establish credibility—a quote from a client or the press may help, for example. But a long-winded account of your company's history will just bore your audience.

- **Emotions.** People are emotional beings. It is not enough to take people through a laundry list of talking points and information on your slides—you must make them *feel* something. There are a million ways to help people feel something about your content. Images are one way to have audiences not only understand your point better, but also feel and have a more visceral and emotional connection to your idea. Explaining the devastation of the Katrina hurricane and floods in the U.S., for example, could be done with bullet points, data, and talking points, but images of the aftermath and the pictures of the human suffering that occurred tell the story in ways that words, text, and data alone never could. Just the words "Hurricane Katrina" conjure up vivid images in your mind. Humans make emotional connections with people, not abstractions. When possible, put your ideas in human terms. "One hundred grams of fat" may seem concrete to you, but for others it is an abstraction. A picture of an enormous plate of greasy French fries, two cheeseburgers, and a large chocolate shake will hit people at a more visceral level. "So that's what 100 grams of fat looks like!"

100 grams of fat

- **Stories.** We tell stories all day long. It's how humans have always communicated. We tell stories with our words and even with our art and music. We express ourselves through the stories we share. We teach, we learn, and we grow through stories. In Japan, it is a custom for a senior worker (*sempai*) to mentor a younger worker (*kohai*) on various issues concerning the company history and culture, and how to do the job. The sempai does much of his informal teaching through storytelling, although nobody calls it that. But that's what it is. Once a younger worker hears the story of what happened to the poor guy who didn't wear his hardhat on the factory floor, he never forgets the lesson (and he never forgets to wear his hardhat). Stories get our attention and are easier to remember than lists of rules. People love Hollywood, Bollywood, and indie films. People are attracted to "story." Why is it, though, that when the majority of smart, talented story-loving people have the chance to present, they usually resort to generating streams of vaguely connected information rather than stories, or examples and illustrations? Great ideas and great presentations have an element of story to them.

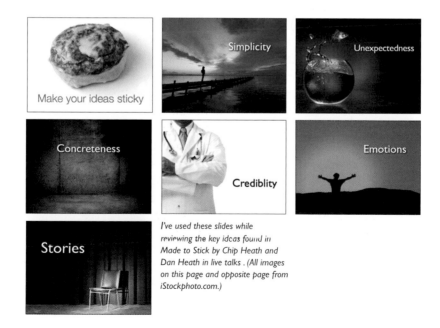

I've used these slides while reviewing the key ideas found in Made to Stick by Chip Heath and Dan Heath in live talks . (All images on this page and opposite page from iStockphoto.com.)

Story and Storytelling

Before there was the written word, humans used stories to transfer culture from one generation to the next. Stories are who we are, and we are our stories. Stories may contain analogies or metaphors, powerful tools for bringing people in and helping them to understand our thoughts clearly and concretely. Good presentations include stories. The best presenters today illustrate their points with stories, often personal ones. The easiest way to explain complicated ideas is through examples or by sharing a story that underscores the point. Stories are easier to recall for your audience. If you want your audience to remember your content, then find a way to make it more relevant and memorable to them by strengthening your core message with good, short, interesting stories or examples.

Good stories have interesting, clear beginnings; provocative, engaging content in the middle; and a clear conclusion. I am not talking about fiction here. I am talking about reality, regardless of the topic. Remember that documentary films, for example, "tell the story" of whatever it is they are reporting on. Documentaries do not simply tell facts, rather they engage us and tell us the story of war, of scientific discovery, of a dramatic sea rescue, of climate change, and so on. We are wired so that we will forget what our brains perceive as unimportant to our survival. Our conscious mind tells us to read the physical chemistry book over and over because we need to pass the class, but our brain keeps telling us that this is dull, uninteresting, and unimportant to our survival. The brain, however, cares about story.

Stories and Authenticity

I have seen pretty good (though not great) presentations that had very average delivery and average graphics, but were relatively effective because the speaker told relevant stories in a clear, concise manner to support his points and in a voice that was human, not formal. Rambling streams of consciousness will not get it done; audiences need to hear (and see) your points illustrated in a real language.

Earlier this year, in fact, I saw a fantastic presentation by the CEO of one of the most famous foreign companies in Japan. The CEO's PowerPoint slides were of mediocre design, and he made the mistake of having not one but two assistants off to the side to advance his slides to match his talk. The assistants seemed to have much difficulty with the slideware and often the wrong slide appeared behind the presenter, but this powerful man simply shrugged his shoulders and said "…ah doesn't matter. My point is…." He moved forward always and captivated the audience with his stories of the firm's past failures and recent successes, stories which contained more captivating and memorable practical business lessons than most business students will get in an entire semester or more.

It is true that the presentation would have been even better if the slides had been better designed and used properly, but in this particular case the CEO gave a powerful and memorable presentation in spite of those shortcomings. Trust me, this is very rare in the world of CEO presentations. There are four essential reasons for his success that night: (1) He knew his material inside and out, and he knew what he wanted to say. (2) He stood front and center and spoke in a real, down-to-earth language that was conversational yet passionate. (3) He did not let technical glitches get in his way. When they occurred, he moved forward without missing a beat, never losing his engagement with the audience. (4) And he used real, sometimes humorous, anecdotes to illustrate his points, and all his stories were supremely poignant and relevant, supporting his core message.

What made this CEO's presentation so compelling and memorable was that it was, above all, authentic. His stories were from his heart and from his gut, not from a memorized script. We do not tell a story from memory alone; we do not need to memorize a story that has meaning to us. If it is real, then it is in us. Based on our research, knowledge, and experience, we can tell it from our gut. Internalize your story, but do not memorize it line by line. You can't fake it. You believe in your story, or you do not. And if you do not, no amount of hyped-up, superficial enthusiasm or conviction will ever make your time with an audience meaningful. If you do not believe it, do not know it to be true, how can you connect and convince others with your words in story form? Your words will be just hollow words.

It's Not Just About Information

People who possess loads of information in a particular field have historically been in hot demand and able to charge high fees for access to their stuffed, fact-filled brains. This was so because the facts used to be difficult to access. Not any more. In an era where information about seemingly anything is only a mouse click away, just possessing information alone is hardly the differentiator it used to be. What is more important today than ever before is the ability to synthesize the facts and give them context and perspective. Picasso once said that "computers are useless for they can only give answers." Computers and Google can indeed give us the routine information and facts that we need. What we want from people who stand before us and give a talk is to give us that which data and information alone cannot: meaning.

Remember that we are living in a time where fundamental human talents are in great demand. Anyone—indeed any machine—can read a list of features or give a stream of facts to an audience. That's not what we need or want. What we yearn for is to listen to an intelligent and evocative—perhaps at times even provocative—human being who teaches us, or inspires us, or who stimulates us with knowledge plus meaning, context, and emotion in a way that is memorable.

And this is where story comes in. Information plus emotion and visualization wrapped in unforgettable anecdotes are the stuff that stories are made of. If presentations were only about following a linear step-by-step formula for distributing information and facts, then no one would be complaining about "death by PowerPoint" today, since the majority of presentations still follow just such a formula. And if designing your slides for your presentation were simply a matter of following a list of rules, do's and don'ts, then why on earth should we keep wasting our time creating slides? Why not simply outsource our facts, outlines, and bullet points to someone who could do it cheaper?

But presentations are not just about following a formula for transferring facts in your head to the heads of those sitting before you by reciting a list of points on a slide. (If it were, why not send an email and cancel the presentation?) What people want is something fundamentally more human. They want to hear "the story" of your facts.

Finding Your Voice

The voice of the storyteller is also important. We pay attention to well-spoken narratives that sound human, that are spoken in a conversational, "human voice." Why do we pay more attention to conversational speech from a storyteller or presenter? It may be because our brain—not our conscious mind—does not know the difference between listening to (or reading) a conversational narrative and actually being in a conversation with a person. When you are in a conversation with someone you are naturally more engaged because you have an obligation to participate. You are involved. Formal speech and formal writing devoid of any emotion whatsoever is extremely difficult to stay with for more than a few minutes. Your conscious mind has to remind you to "stay awake, this is important!" But someone who speaks in a natural, human, conversational style is far easier to stay engaged with.

Majora Carter speaks with a "human voice" at the TED Conference in 2005, explaining her fight for environmental justice in the South Bronx. (TED/ leslieimage.com)

Dana Atchley (1941-2000)
A Digital Storytelling Pioneer

Dana Atchley was a legend and pioneer in the field of digital storytelling. His clients included Coke, EDS, Adobe, Silicon Graphics, and many others. He even worked with Apple as a charter member of the AppleMasters program. In the '90s, Atchley was helping senior executives create emotional, compelling talks that used the latest technology to create "digital stories" that connected and appealed to audiences in a more visceral, visual, emotional, and memorable way. If Atchley had not sadly passed away at age 59 in 2000, presentations—even in the world of business—might be far more appropriate, engaging, and effective today. Here's what Dana Atchley said about digital storytelling:

> "...digital storytelling combines the best of two worlds: the 'new world' of digitized video, photography and art, and the 'old world' of telling stories. This means the 'old world' of PowerPoint slides filled with bullet point statements will be replaced by a 'new world' of examples via stories, accompanied by evocative images and sounds."

Here's what Dan Pink, writing for *FastCompany*, said about Dana Atchley and his mission in this excerpt from his 1999 article called "What's Your Story?"

> "...[W]hy does communication about business remain so tedious? Most businesspeople describe their dreams and strategies—their stories—just as they've been doing it for decades: stiffly, from behind a podium, and maybe with a few slides. Call it 'Corporate Sominex.' Digital storytelling is more than a technique. In fact, it's become something of a movement among both artists and businesspeople."

This bit from the *FastCompany* article makes the future of business presentations sound so promising. I get excited reading this and thinking about the possibilities. Yet, since 1999, how much has really changed? Nine years have passed. Some people today are indeed using digital technology in presentations the way Atchley envisioned. But there is such a long, long way to go before we rid the business world of the "corporate Sominex" phenomenon.

Learn more about Dana Winslow Atchley III and his brilliant contributions on the Next Exit Web site.

www.nextexit.com

The Process

The problem with slideware applications—PowerPoint, in particular, since it's been around longer and influenced a generation—is that they have, by default, guided users toward presenting in outline form with subject titles and bullet points grouped under each topic heading. This is similar to the ol' topic sentence in the high school composition class. Seems logical enough, but it is a structure that makes the delivery of the content utterly forgettable for the audience. Storyboarding can help. If you take the time in this part of the preparation stage and set your ideas up in a logical fashion in storyboard format, you can then visualize the sequential movement of your content narrative and the overall flow and "feel" of the presentation.

Since you have already identified your core message away from the computer, you can now begin to create a storyboard that will begin to give shape to the story of your short presentation. Storyboards have their origins in the movie industry, but are used often in business, particularly in the field of marketing and advertising.

One of the simplest and most useful features of PowerPoint and Keynote is the Slide Sorter view (Light Table view in Keynote). You can take your notes and sketches and create a storyboard directly in PowerPoint or Keynote, or you can remain "analog" a bit longer and draft a storyboard on paper or by using Post-its or a whiteboard, etc.

Each situation and each individual is different, and there are indeed many paths to better presentations, including better preparation. My personal approach moving from rough analog sketches to digital slides is not uncommon at all. Many people take a similar approach. I have been surprised, however, that for the most part today individual professionals, entrepreneurs, and students usually just open up PowerPoint and type about a dozen subject slides and then fill them with talking points. This is not an effective approach, nor is it a method I recommend, although it is common.

Below is the four-step approach I usually take. I sometimes skip the third step, but I find it works well when a group is planning the presentation. For students working on a group presentation, Step 3 is vital.

Step 1

Brainstorming. Step back, go analog, get away from the computer, tap into the right brain and brainstorm ideas. I do not edit ideas much here; the aim is to just let it flow. I explore. It may be messy. That's OK. What I'm tying to do—whether I am working alone or leading a group—is to see the issue from all sides. But to do that, you have to take a step back and see the big picture. When I work with a client, I listen carefully and ask questions. I listen far more than I speak. The listening is the important part. I'll look for themes in Step 2, although if clear themes are emerging as I listen and probe, then I'll begin to group items as we go.

Brainstorming "off the grid" away from the computer.

Step 2

Grouping & identifying the core. In this step, I look to identify the one key idea that is central (and memorable) from the point of view of the audience. What is the "it" that I want them to get? I use "chunking" to group similar ideas while looking for a unifying theme. The presentation may be organized into three parts, so first I look for the central theme that will be the thread running through the presentation. There is no rule that says your presentation should have three sections or three "acts" from the world of drama. However, three is a good number to aim for because it is a manageable constraint and generally provides a memorable structure. Regardless of how many sections I use, there is only one theme. It all comes back to supporting that key message. The supporting structure—the three parts—is there to back up the core message and the story.

The core "takeaway" and theme are identified and the talk is organized into three concrete sections.

Step 3

Storyboarding off the computer. I take the ideas sketched out on paper in Step 2 and lay them out with Post-it notes. The advantage of this method (compared to the Slide Sorter view in PowerPoint or the Light Table view in Keynote) is that I can easily add content by writing on an additional Post-it and sticking it under the appropriate section without ever losing sight of the structure and flow. In software I have to switch to Slide mode to type or add an image directly on a slide and then go back to the Slide Sorter mode to see the big-picture structure. Alternatively—and this is very popular with my Japanese business students—you can print out blank slides, 12 slides per sheet, which gives you essentially a larger version of a Moleskine Storyboard. If you want larger slides, you can print out nine slides or six. You then can tape these to the wall or spread them out on the desk, keeping them in a notebook when you're done. As shown below, you can sketch your visuals and write down your key points in a printed version of slideware notes.

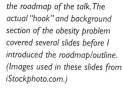

Actual slides. Shown here are the title slide, the "hook," and the roadmap of the talk. The actual "hook" and background section of the obesity problem covered several slides before I introduced the roadmap/outline. (Images used in these slides from iStockphoto.com.)

Rough sketches of slides in blank printouts from PowerPoint.

Step 4

Storyboarding in Slide Sorter/Light Table view. If you have a clear sense of your structure, you can skip Step 3 and start building the flow of your presentation directly in slideware. Create a blank slide using a template of your choosing (or the simplest version of your company's template if you must use it). I usually choose a blank slide and then place a simple text box inside it with the size and font I'll use most often. (You can create multiple master slides in PowerPoint and Keynote.) Then I duplicate several of these slides, since they will contain the visual content of my presentation, short sentences or single words, images, quotes, charts & graphs, etc. The section slides—what presentations guru Jerry Weismann calls *bumper slides*—should be a different color with enough contrast that they stand out when you see them in the slide sorter view. You can have these slides hidden so that you see them only when planning in Slide Sorter view if you prefer; however, in my case, these slides will serve to give visual closure to one section and open the next section.

Now that I have a simple structure in the Slide Sorter view, I can add visuals that support my narrative. I have an introduction where I introduce the issue or "the pain" and introduce the core message. I then use the next three sections to support my assertions or "solve the pain" in a way that is interesting and informative but that never loses sight of the simple core message.

For detailed advice about creating your story using the Slide Sorter view, I recommend Cliff Atkinson's *Beyond Bullet Points* (Microsoft Press).

ABOVE *Rough outline from Step Two for a presentation I created on presentation design.*

RIGHT *The start of the storyboarding process in Step Four for the same presentation. The total number of slides used was over 150 for the talk, but here you can see the simple structure before slides were added to the appropriate sections.*

Nancy Duarte

CEO of Duarte Design, the world's leading presentation design firm. Clients include Al Gore and the biggest companies in Silicon Valley and beyond.
www.duarte.com

Nancy Duarte talks about storyboards and the process of presentation design.

Much of our communication today exhibits the quality of intangibility. Services, software, causes, thought leadership, change management, company vision—they're often more conceptual than concrete, more ephemeral than firm. And there's nothing wrong with that. But we regularly struggle when communicating these types of ideas because they are essentially invisible. It's difficult to share one's vision when there's nothing to see. Expressing these invisible ideas visually, so that they feel tangible and actionable, is a bit of an art form, and the best place to start is not with the computer. A pencil and a sheet of paper will do nicely.

Why take this seemingly Luddite approach? Because presentation software was never intended to be a brainstorming or drawing tool. The applications are simply containers for ideas and assets, not the means to generate them. Too many of us have fallen into the trap of launching our presentation applications to prepare our content. In reality, the best creative process requires stepping away from technology and relying on the same tools of expression we grew up with—pens, pencils, crayons if you're into hardcore regression. The goal is to generate ideas—not necessarily pictures yet— but lots of ideas. These can be words, diagrams or scenes; they can be literal or metaphorical; the only requirement is that they express your underlying thoughts. The best thing about this process is that you don't need to figure out how to use drawing tools or where to save the file. Everything you

need you already have (and don't say you can't draw; you're just out of practice). This means you can generate a large quantity of ideas in a relatively short amount of time. And that's what we're going for right now: quantity.

For me, one idea per sticky note is preferable. And I use a Sharpie. The reason? If it takes more space than a Post-it and requires more detail than a Sharpie can provide, the idea is too complex. Simplicity is the essence of clear communication. Additionally, sticky notes make it easy to arrange and re-arrange content until the structure and flow feels right. On the other hand, many people on my team use a more traditional storyboarding approach, preferring to linearly articulate detailed ideas. That's fine, too. The point is not to prescribe exactly how to work, but to encourage you to generate a lot of ideas and to do so quickly.

Often ideas come immediately. That's good, but avoid the potential pitfall of going with the first thing that comes to mind. Continue to sketch and force yourself to think through several more ideas. It takes discipline and tenacity—especially when it feels like you solved it on the first try. Explore words and word associations to generate several ideas. Use mind mapping and word-storming techniques to create yet more ideas (digital natives might prefer mind mapping software for this phase). Stronger solutions frequently appear after four or five ideas have percolated to the top. Continue generating ideas even if they seem to wander down unrelated paths; you never know what you might find, after all. Then, once you've generated an enormous amount of ideas, identify a handful that meet the objective of the vision or concept you're trying to communicate. It matters less what form they take at this point than that they get your message across.

By the way, cheesy metaphors are a cop-out. If you feel tempted to use a picture of two hands shaking in front of a globe, put the pencil down, step away from the desk, and think about taking a vacation or investigating aromatherapy. Push yourself to generate out-of-the-box ideas. Take the time and spend the creative energy because the payoff will be a presentation people not only remember, but one they take action on.

Now, begin to sketch pictures from the ideas. These sketches become visual triggers that spark more ideas. The sketching process should be loose and quick—doodles really. Search through stock houses, magazines, even YouTube for images and vignettes to reference while sketching. Generate as many pictures as you can, and while that's happening start to think about layout to ensure that the elements work spatially on a slide. In this way, sketching serves as proof-of-concept because ideas that are too complex or time consuming or costly will present themselves as ripe for elimination. Don't worry about throwing things away—that's why you generated a lot of ideas in the first place. In fact, you're ultimately going to have to throw all of them away except for one (designers recognize this as the destructive aspect of the creative process; it's a good thing).

Some of the ideas you generate may require multiple scenes built across a few slides versus a snapshot on a single slide. On the other hand, sometimes it's as simple as using the perfect picture or diagram. Getting your great idea across might require that you manipulate an image, create a custom illustration or produce a short video. Focus on whatever works best, not on the idea that's easiest to execute. Now, find a colleague and walk them through your sketches. Have them give you feedback on what works best in the context of your audience and personal style. They'll likely have insights that will improve your idea.

Here's where it gets a bit more difficult. Depending on the concept you've identified as the one best suited to convey your idea, you may or may not have the skills to execute the idea digitally. Be prepared to enlist the help of a designer (you did plan far enough ahead to make sure you've got one available, right?) There's no shame in seeking professional help, after all; what's important is effective communication, regardless of whether or not you have the skill set to execute it.

Insider Tip 1: If you prefer the storyboarding approach, streamline it by creating six blank text slides in your master template. Print them out as 6-up handouts and you'll have a master storyboard sheet with miniature blank slides in the correct aspect ratio. Each slide contains the graphical background elements from your template, and anything you sketch would be within the framework of any visual brand elements in your template.

Insider Tip 2: When sketching for a client, it's important to listen to what they say, but it's more important to identify the underlying intent of what they didn't say. Sketch while they talk so they can see how their words are being interpreted. Try to sketch three unique ideas that accurately reflect their content.

Brainstorming with Nancy Duarte (far left) and two of her staff, Paula and Victoria, in the head office of Duarte Design in Silicon Valley.

ANALIST

DEFINE

DESIGN

DEVELOP

TEST

DEPLOY

Sample sketches (opposite page and below) from Duarte Design giving a glimpse of how pros refine the visualization of their ideas on paper before creating slides in software.

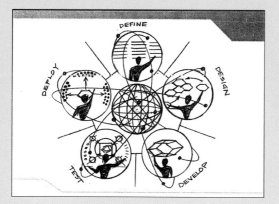

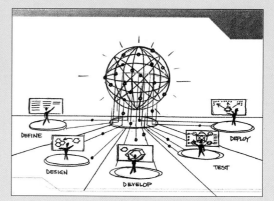

Finished slides in digital form.

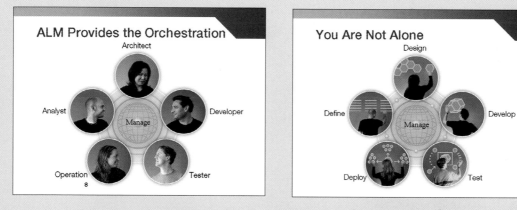

If you feel tempted to use a picture of two hands shaking in front of a globe, put the pencil down, step away from the desk, and think about taking a vacation or investigating aromatherapy.

—Nancy Duarte

Editing and Restraint

I am a bit of a Star Wars geek. Over the years, as I've learned more about the incredible creativity (and hard work) behind Lucas's films, I realized that we mere mortals can learn much about presentations (which are essentially opportunities to tell our story) by listening to the advice of master storytellers like George Lucas, and others.

As I researched the numerous interviews over the years of Lucas talking about the making of the Star Wars films, one key idea often discussed was the importance of editing like mad to get the story down to about two hours. To do this, they scrutinized every scene to make sure that the scene—no matter how cool it was—actually contributed to the story. If during the editing process a scene was judged to be superfluous to the story in any way, it was cut (or trimmed, if the length was the only problem). They were very keen on keeping to the two-hour format because this was in the best interest of the audience.

We have all seen scenes from movies that left us scratching our heads wondering how they contributed to the story. Perhaps the director felt the scene was so technically cool or so difficult to make that he just couldn't stand the thought of not including it in the film. But that would be a poor reason to include a scene. As far as presentations go, we also have all seen people include data, facts, or graphics, or a seemingly unrelated anecdote that just did not contribute to the speaker's overall point (which we were probably at a loss to find anyway). Presenters often include superfluous items because they are perhaps proud of their work and want to show it off, even if it really did not help support the speaker's particular point.

Moral of the story: always keep the audience in mind by first keeping your talk as short as you can and still doing an effective job telling your story, and second, after you have prepared your presentation, go back and edit like crazy, eliminating parts that are not absolutely crucial to your overall point or purpose of the talk. You must be ruthless. When in doubt, cut it out.

It's paramount that we be ruthless editors of our own material. We have to make the tough choices, choosing even not do something (because it is not meeting your standards, for example). The hardest thing can be deciding to cut and even abandon material altogether, but it must be done.

Many people are not good at editing their presentations because they are afraid. They figure that nobody ever got fired for including too much information. Better safe than sorry, they say. But this leads to lots of material and wasted time. Covering your butt by including every thing under the sun is not the right place to be coming from; it's not the most appropriate motivation. It is after all only a presentation and no matter how much you include, someone will always say, "hey why didn't you say_____!" Difficult people are out there, but don't play to them and do not let fear guide your decisions.

Designing a tight presentation which has the facts right but does so by giving simple, concrete anecdotes that touch people's emotions is not easy work, but it's worth it. Every successful presentation has elements of story to it. Your job is to identify the elements of your content that can be organized in a way that tells a memorable story.

In Sum

- Make your ideas sticky by keeping things simple, using examples and stories, looking for the unexpected, and tapping into people's emotions.

- A presentation is never *just* about the facts.

- Brainstorm your topic away from the computer, chunk (group) the most important bits. Identify the underlying theme and be true to that theme (core message) throughout the creation of the presentation.

- Make a storyboard of your ideas on paper—and then use software to lay out a solid structure that you can see.

- Show restraint at all times and bring everything back to the core message.

design

**Our lives are frittered away by detail;
simplify, simplify.**

— Henry David Thoreau

5

Simplicity:
Why It Matters

As our daily lives have become more complex, more and more people look to incorporate simplicity into their lives. But finding simplicity in the workplace seems harder these days, not easier. Professionally, people are terrified of being simple for fear of being labeled a lightweight. So "when in doubt, add more" is often the guiding principle.

There is a fundamental misunderstanding of simplicity and what it means to be simple today. Many people confuse simple, for example, with simplistic and simplism or that which is dumbed-down to the point of being deceptive or misleading. "Simple" to some people means necessarily a kind of oversimplification of an issue, which ignores complexities and creates obfuscation and outright falsehoods. Politicians are often guilty of this type of oversimplification. But this is not the kind of simplicity I am talking about here. The kind of simplicity I am talking about does not come from a place of laziness or ignorance, rather it comes from an intelligent desire for clarity that gets to the essence of an issue, something which is not easy to do. Simplicity is not easy, in fact, it is hard.

Simplicity—along with other precepts such as restraint and naturalness—are key ideas found in Zen and the Zen arts. Arts like the tea ceremony, haiku, ikebana, and sumi-e, which can take many years, or indeed, a lifetime to master. There is nothing easy about them, although when performed by a master, they may seem beautifully simple. It is difficult to give a definition of simplicity, but when I say we need to create messages and design visuals that are simple, I am not talking about taking shortcuts, or ignoring complexities, or endorsing meaningless sound bytes and shallow content. When I use the word simple (or simplicity), I am referring to the term as being essentially synonymous with clarity, directness, subtlety, essentialness, and minimalism. Designers, such as interaction designers, for example, are constantly looking for the simplest solution to complex problems. The simple solutions are not necessarily easiest for them, but the results may end up being the "easiest" to use for the end user.

The best visuals are often ones designed with an eye toward simplicity. Yet, this says nothing about the specifics of a visual presentation. That will depend on the content and context. For example, even the best visuals used in support of a presentation for one audience on, say, quantum mechanics, may appear complicated and confusing to a different audience. Simplicity is often used as a means to greater clarity. However, simplicity can also be viewed as a consequence. A consequence, that is, of our careful efforts to craft a story and create supporting visuals that focus on our audience's needs in a clear and meaningful way.

Simplicity is an important design principle, but simplicity itself is not a panacea. Though people usually err on the side of making presentation slides more complicated than they need to be, it is indeed possible to be "too simple." Simplicity is the goal, but as Einstein said, "Make everything as simple as possible but no simpler."

Steve Jobs and the Zen Aesthetic

Apple co-founder and CEO Steve Jobs is one of the best presenters in the world of business today. Jobs is clear and to the point. His presentations generate a lot of positive buzz and always release yet another wave of viral communication about the presentation's content. This happens in part because the content is easily grasped and remembered by both the media and regular customers. You can't "spread the word" if you don't get what the word is. With Jobs's public presentations, there is both a verbal and visual clarity. This is what great leaders do. Ben McConnell and Jackie Huba, authors of *Creating Customer Evangelists* (Kaplan Business) make a good observation about Jobs:

> *"Jobs does just what a leader is supposed to do: Provide a vision of where the company ship is headed and make sure everyone understands it."*

Part of Jobs's great clarity can be seen even in the slides that accompany his talks. I am stretching things a bit here, but there is almost a "Zen aesthetic" to Steve Jobs's presentation visuals. In Jobs's slides you can see evidence of restraint, simplicity, and powerful yet subtle use of empty space.

Bill Gates, one of the most powerful and philanthropic businessmen of our time, provides a lesson in contrast. In a typical presentation with slides, Gates and his staff do what millions of other PowerPoint users do daily—they use PowerPoint in a way that does not help their cause. The problems with Gates's slides are all too common: too many elements on one slide, over use of bullet points (including long lines of text), cheesy-looking images, too many colors, overused gradation (even the text has gradation), weak visual communication priority, and an overall impression of clutter on-screen.

Both Steve Jobs and Bill Gates use slides to complement their talks. The biggest difference, however, is that Jobs's visuals are a big part of his talk. The visuals do not overpower him but they are a *necessary component* of the talk, not just ornamentation or notes to remind him what to say. Jobs uses the slides to help him tell a story and he interacts with them in a natural way, rarely turning his back on the audience. Jobs uses the huge backlit screen behind him in the same spirit at least that George Lucas uses the screen: to help tell a story. Lucas uses actors, visuals, and effects to convey his message, Jobs uses visuals and his own words and natural presence to tell his story. Jobs's slides flow smoothly with his talk.

In Bill Gates's case the slides are often not only of low aesthetic quality, they simply do not really help the Chairman's narrative very much. Bill's slides are often not really necessary; they are more of an ornament or a decoration off to the side. In many instances Bill Gates would be better off just pulling up a stool and sharing his ideas and then answering questions that audience members could have submitted before the talk so that he could select which he would answer. You don't have to use slideware for every presentation, but if you do, the visuals should seem a part of the show, not something "over there" off to the side.

I like Bill Gates a lot and from what people at Microsoft tell me, he's also a nice guy and a pleasure to speak with. One on one he's engaging. But when it comes to his public keynote presentations—and the visuals that accompany those talks—there is much he could learn about "presenting differently" from Steve Jobs. Bill Gates's keynotes are not terrible, they are just very average and unremarkable. His PowerPoint-driven style is "normal" and "typical" and his presentations are largely unmemorable as a result. Bill Gates is a remarkable man, his presentations should be remarkable too.

If you are going to get up in front of a lot of people and say that the design of your strategy matters and that the design of your integrated software matters, then at the very least the visuals you use—right here and right now, at this moment in time with this particular audience—also need to be the result of thoughtful design, not hurried decoration.

Photo courtesy of Gail Murphy

Photo courtesy of Christoph Dernbach
(www.mr-gadget.de)

Kanso, Shizen, Shibumi

Zen itself is not concerned with judging this design to be "good" or that design to be "bad." Still, we can look to some of the concepts in the Zen aesthetic to help us improve our own visuals with an eye toward simplicity.

Kanso (Simplicity)

A key tenet of the Zen aesthetic is kanso or simplicity. In the kanso concept, beauty and visual elegance are achieved by elimination and omission. Says artist, designer, and architect, Dr. Koichi Kawana, "Simplicity means the achievement of maximum effect with minimum means." When you examine your visuals, then, can you say that you are getting the maximum impact with a minimum of graphic elements, for example? When you take a look at Jobs's slides and Gates's slides, how do they compare for kanso?

Shizen (Naturalness)

The aesthetic concept of naturalness or shizen "prohibits the use of elaborate designs and over refinement," according to Dr. Kawana. Restraint is a beautiful thing. Talented jazz musicians, for example, know never to overplay but instead to be forever mindful of the other musicians and find their own space within the music and within the moment they are sharing. Graphic designers show restraint by including only what is necessary to communicate the particular message for the particular audience. Restraint is hard. Complication and elaboration are easy… and are common. The suggestive mode of expression is a key Zen aesthetic. Dr. Kawana, commenting on the design of traditional Japanese gardens, says: "The designer must adhere to the concept of *miegakure* since Japanese believe that in expressing the whole the interest of the viewer is lost."

Shibumi (Elegance)

Shibumi is a principle that can be applied to many aspects of life. Concerning visual communication and graphic design, shibumi represents elegant simplicity and articulate brevity, an understated elegance. In *Wabi-Sabi Style*, (Gibbs Smith Publishers), authors James and Sandra Crowley comment on the Japanese deep appreciation of beauty in this sense:

"Their (Japanese) conceptualization relegates elaborate ornamentation and vivid color usage to the bottom of the taste levels… excess requires no real thought or creativity. The highest level of taste moves beyond the usage of brilliant colors and heavy ornamentation to a simple and subdued refinement that is the beauty of shibumi, which represents the ultimate in good taste through conscious reserve. This is the original 'less is more' concept. Less color—subdued and elegant usage of color, less clutter…"

In the world of slide presentations, you do not always need to visually spell everything out. You do not need to pound every detail into the head of each member of your audience either visually or verbally. Instead, the combination of your words, along with the visual images you project, should motivate the viewer and arouse his imagination, helping him to empathize with your idea and visualize your idea far beyond what is visible in the ephemeral PowerPoint slide before him. The Zen aesthetic values include (but are not limited to):

- Simplicity
- Subtlety
- Elegance
- Suggestive rather than the descriptive or obvious
- Naturalness (i.e., nothing artificial or forced),
- Empty space (or negative space)
- Stillness, Tranquility
- Eliminating the nonessential

All of these principles can be applied to slide design, Web design, and so on.

Wabi-Sabi Simplicity

I first learned of wabi-sabi while studying *sado* (Japanese tea ceremony) many years ago in the Shimokita Hanto of Aomori, a rural part of northern Japan—a perfect place to experience traditional Japanese values and concepts. While studying sado, I began to appreciate the aesthetic simplicity of the ritual, an art that is an expression of fundamental Zen principles such as purity, tranquility, and a respect for nature and the desire to live in harmony with it.

The ideals of wabi-sabi come from Japan, and the origins are based on keen observations of nature. Wabi literally means "poverty" or lacking material wealth and all its possessions, yet at the same time feeling free from depending on worldly things, including social status. There is an inward feeling of something higher. Sabi means "loneliness" or "solitude," the feeling you might have while walking alone on a deserted beach... deep in contemplation. These two concepts come together to give us an appreciation for the grace and beauty of a scene or a work of art, while remaining fully aware of its ephemerality and impermanence.

Some Westerners may be familiar with the term wabi-sabi through wabi-sabi-inspired design, a kind of earthy interior design which is balanced, organic, free from clutter and chaos, and somehow quite beautiful in its simple presentation, never appearing ostentatious or decorated.

The ideals of wabi-sabi are most applicable to such disciplines as architecture, interior design, and the fine arts. But we can apply the principles to the art of digital storytelling (presentations with AV support/integration) as well. Wabi-sabi embraces the "less is more" idea that is often talked about and often ignored in today's society. Visuals created with a sense of wabi-sabi are ones which are never accidental, arbitrary, cluttered, or busy.

They may be beautiful, perhaps, but never superfluous or decorative. They will be harmonious and balanced, whether symmetrical or asymmetrical. The elimination of distraction and noise can certainly help begin to make visuals with greater clarity.

A Zen garden is also a lesson in simplicity. Open space without ornamentation, a few rocks carefully selected and placed, raked gravel. Beautiful. Simple. The Zen garden is very different from many gardens in the West that are absolutely filled with beauty, so much beauty, in fact, that we miss much of it. Presentations are a bit like this. Sometimes, we're presented with so much visual and auditory stimulation in such a short time that we end up understanding very little and remembering even less. We witnessed a large quantity of "stuff," but what of the quality? Is it not the quality of the evidence and the experience that matters, rather than, say, merely the amount of data or the length of the experience?

Living here in Japan all these years, I have had many chances to experience the Zen aesthetic, either while visiting a garden, practicing zazen in a Kyoto temple, or even while having a traditional Japanese meal out with friends. I am convinced that a visual approach which embraces the aesthetic concepts of simplicity and the removal of the nonessential can have practical applications in our professional lives and can lead ultimately to a more enlightened design. I do not suggest you judge a presentation visual the same way you do a work of art, of course. But understanding the essence of Zen simplicity can have practical applications in your creative work, including the design of your presentation visuals.

The "Fish Story"

After I presented for a large tech company in Silicon Valley, I received this note below from Deepak, an engineer in the audience. This little story illustrates the idea of reducing the nonessential.

Dear Garr... When you talked about reducing the text on the slides, I was reminded of a story from my childhood in India. If I remember it right, it goes like this:

> When Vijay opened his store, he put up a sign that said: "We Sell Fresh Fish Here." His father stopped by and said that the word "We" suggests an emphasis on the seller rather than the customer, and is really not needed. So the sign was changed to "Fresh Fish Sold Here."
>
> His brother came by and suggested that the word "here" could be done away with—it was superfluous. Vijay agreed and changed the sign to "Fresh Fish Sold."
>
> Next, his sister came along and said the sign should just say "Fresh Fish." Clearly, it is being sold; what else could you be doing?
>
> Later, his neighbor stopped by to congratulate him. Then he mentioned that all passers-by could easily tell that the fish was really fresh. Mentioning the word fresh actually made it sound defensive as though there was room for doubt about the freshness. Now the sign just read: "FISH."
>
> As Vijay was walking back to his shop after a break he noticed that one could identify the fish from its smell from very far, at a distance from which one could barely read the sign. He knew there was no need for the word "FISH."

By stripping down an image to essential meaning, an artist can amplify that meaning...

—Scott McCloud

Amplification Through Simplification

The Japanese Zen arts teach us that it is possible to express great beauty and convey powerful messages through simplification. Zen may not verbalize "amplification through simplification," but you can see this idea everywhere in the Zen-inspired arts. There is a style of Japanese painting called the "one-corner" style, for example, which goes back some 800 years and is derived from concepts of wabi and sabi. Paintings in this style are very simple and contain much empty space. You may have a painting depicting a large ocean scene and empty sky, for example. In the corner, there is a small, old fishing canoe, hardly visible. It's the smallness and placement of the canoe that gives vastness to the ocean and evokes at once a feeling of calm and an empathy for the aloneness the fisherman faces. Such visuals have few elements, yet can be profoundly evocative.

Learning From the Art of Comics

We can learn about simplicity as it relates to presentation visuals from unexpected places, including—and this may surprise you—the art of comics. And the best place to learn about the art of comics is from Scott McCloud's *Understanding Comics: The Invisible Art* (Harper Paperbacks). In this popular book, McCloud repeatedly touches on the idea of "amplification through simplification." McCloud says that cartooning is a form of amplification through simplification because the abstract images in comics are not so much the elimination of detail as they are an effort to focus on specific details.

A key feature of many comics is their visual simplicity. Yet, as McCloud reminds us, while casting an eye to the wonderful world of Japanese comics, "simple style does not necessitate simple story." Many people (outside of Japan at least) prejudge comics by their simple lines and forms as being necessarily simplistic and base, perhaps suitable for children and "the lazy," but not something that could possibly have depth and intelligence. Surely such a simple style found in comics cannot be illustrating a complex story they say.

However, if you visit coffee shops around Tokyo University—Japan's most elite university—you will see stacks and stacks of comics (*manga*) on the shelves. There is nothing necessarily "stupid" about the genre of comics in Japan at all; in fact, you'll find "brainiacs" in all shapes and sizes reading comics here, and indeed around the world.

The situation today is that most people have not been exposed to the idea of making a visual stronger by stripping it down to its essence. Less always equals less in most people's eyes. If we apply this visual illiteracy to the world of presentations, you can imagine the frustration that a young "enlightened" professional must feel when her boss looks over her presentation visuals the day before her big presentation and says, "No good. Too simple. You haven't said anything with these slides! Where are your bullet points!? Where's the company logo!? You're wasting space—put some data in there!" She tries to explain that the slides are not the presentation but that she is the presentation and that the "points" will be coming from her mouth. She tries to explain that the slides contain a delicate balance of text and images and data designed to play a supportive yet powerful role in helping her amplify her message. She attempts to remind her boss that they also have strong, detailed documentation for the client and that slides and documents are not the same. But her boss will have none of it. The boss is not happy until the "PowerPoint deck" looks like "normal PowerPoints," you know, the kind used by "serious people."

We must do what we can to be firm, however, and remain open to the idea of "amplification through simplification" as much as possible. I am not suggesting that you become an artist or that you should draw your own images. Rather, I am suggesting that you can learn a lot about how to present images and words together by exploring the so-called "low art" of comics. In fact, although presentation visuals were surely the farthest thing from McCloud's mind when he wrote the book, we can learn far more about effective communication for the conceptual age from McCloud's book than we can from many books on PowerPoint. For example, early in the book McCloud builds a definition of comics and finally arrives with this, a definition he admits is not written in stone:

> *"Juxtaposed pictorial and other images in deliberate sequence intended to convey information and/or to produce an aesthetic response in the viewer."*

It is easy to imagine, with some tweaking, how this could be applied to other storytelling media and presentation contexts as well. We do not have a good definition for "live presentation with slides," but a great presentation may indeed contain slides that are comprised of "juxtaposed pictorial and other images." And great presentations certainly have elements of sequence designed to "convey information and/or to produce an aesthetic response."

At the end of the book, McCloud gives us some simple, Zen-like wisdom. He's talking about writers, artists, and the art of comics, but this is good advice to live by no matter where our creative talents may lie. "All that's needed," he says, "...is the desire to be heard. The will to learn. And the ability to see."

When you get right down to it, it always comes back to desire, a willingness to learn, and the ability to really see. Many of us have the desire; it's the learning and seeing that's the hard part. McCloud says that in order for us to understand comics, we need to "...clear our minds of all preconceived notions about comics. Only by starting from scratch can we discover the full range of possibilities comics offer." The same can be said for presentation design. Only by approaching presentations and presentation design with a completely open mind can we see the options before us. It is just a matter of seeing.

Redux: Simplicity Is Not Easy

Usually, we think about time in terms of "How can I save more time?" Time is a constraint for us, but when planning a presentation, what if we took the notion of "timesaving" and looked at it from the point of view of our audience instead of our own personal desires to do things more quickly and save time? What if it wasn't just about *our time,* but it was about *their time*? When I am in the audience, I appreciate it very much when I am in the presence of a speaker who is engaged, has done his homework, has prepared compelling visuals which add rather than bore, and generally makes me happy I have attended. What I hate more than anything—and I know you do too—is the feeling I get when I realize I am at the beginning of a wasted hour ahead of me.

Often, the approach I advocate may use more time, not less time, for you to prepare, but the time you are saving for your audience can be huge. Again, the question is: Is it always about saving time for ourselves? Isn't it important to save time for others? When I save time for myself, I am pleased. But when I save time for my audience—by not only *not* wasting their time but instead by sharing something important with them—I feel inspired, energized, and rewarded.

I can save time on the front end, but I may waste more time for others on the back end. For example, if I give a completely worthless one-hour death-by-PowerPoint presentation to an audience of 200, that equals 200 hours of wasted time. But if I instead put in the time, say, 25–30 hours or more of planning and designing the message, and the media, then I can give the world 200 hours of a worthwhile, memorable experience.

Software companies advertise time-saving features, which may help us believe we have saved time to complete a task such as preparing a presentation and "simplified" our workday. But if time is not saved for the audience—if the audience wastes its time because we didn't prepare well, design the visuals well, or perform well—then what does it matter that we saved one hour in preparing our slides? Doing things in less time sometimes does indeed feel simpler, but if it results in wasted time and wasted opportunities later, it is hardly simple.

In Sum

- Simplicity is powerful and leads to greater clarity, yet it is neither simple nor easy to achieve.

- Simplicity can be obtained through the careful reduction of the nonessential.

- As you design slides, keep the following concepts in mind: subtlety, grace, and understated elegance.

- Good designs have plenty of empty space. Think "subtract" not "add."

- While simplicity is the goal, it is possible to be "too simple." Your job is to find the balance most appropriate to your situation.

6

Presentation Design: Principles and Techniques

When I was an employee with Sumitomo in the mid-90s, I discovered that Japanese business people often used the term "case-by-case" (*keisu bai keisu*) when discussing details of future events or strategy. This frustrated me since I was used to more concrete plans and absolutes and making decisions rather quickly. I learned, though, that context, circumstance, and a kind of "particularism" were very important to the Japanese with whom I worked. Today, I might use Japanese expressions like *jyoukyou ni yotte* (judgment depends on circumstance) or *toki to baai ni yotte* (depends on time and circumstance) when discussing what techniques or designs to use for a particular presentation, for example. I used to think that "it depends" was a weak statement, a cop-out of sorts. Now I see that it is wise. Without a good knowledge of the place and circumstance, and the content and context of a presentation, it is difficult to say this is "appropriate" and that is "inappropriate" necessarily, let alone to judge what is "good" or "bad." There are no cookie-cutter approaches to design. Graphic design is as much art as science.

Nonetheless, there are some general guidelines that most appropriate and strong slide designs share. There are a few basic and fundamental concepts and design principles that if properly understood, can indeed help the average person create presentation visuals that are far more effective. One could fill several volumes with design principles and techniques. In this chapter, though, I'll exercise restraint and elaborate on just a few principles along with practical examples and a few techniques. First, let's look at what is meant by design.

Presentation Design

A common misunderstanding about design is that it is something that comes at the end, for example, it's the frosting and "Happy Birthday!" on a cake. But this is not what I mean by design. For me, design does not come at the end; rather, it comes at the beginning, right from the start. Design is necessary and a way to organize information in a way that makes things clearer; it is also a medium for persuasion. Design can make things easier for the viewer or the user. Design is not decoration.

If anything, design is more about subtraction than addition. Visually, we do not want to include too much, nor do we want to exclude too much. Generally, people err on the side of including too much visual information, which often results in clutter and confusion. Stephen M. Kosslyn, a Harvard professor and author of *Clear and to the Point: 8 Psychological Principles for Compelling PowerPoint Presentations* (Oxford University Press), warns against the inclusion of too much or too little: "It might be tempting to show how smart, knowledgeable, and well-prepared you are by showering the audience with details. But if that information doesn't really help you tell your story, and doesn't help the audience understand your main points, then it just gets in the way. You will force the audience members to search for the information-bearing needle in the haystack of your words and graphics—and they will probably just give up."

In the world of design, there is more than one solution to a single problem. You need to explore, but ultimately you need to look for the most appropriate solution for the problem, given the context of your information. Design is about making conscious decisions about inclusion and exclusion.

General Design Principles

In the following sections, I'll take you through seven interconnected design principles that are fundamental to good slide design. The first two—Signal vs. Noise Ratio and Picture Superiority Effect—are quite broad concepts but with practical applications to slide design. The third —Empty Space—helps us look at slides in a different way and appreciate the power of what is not included to make visual messages stronger. The final four principles are grouped together in what I call "the big four" of basic design principles: Contrast, Repetition, Alignment, and Proximity. Designer and author Robin Williams also applied these four basic principles to the art of document design in her best-selling book *The Non-Designer's Design Book* (Peachpit Press). I'll show you how the principles can be applied to improving slide design.

Signal vs Noise Ratio

The Signal-to-Noise Ratio (SNR) is a principle borrowed from more technical fields such as radio communications and electronic communication in general, but the principle itself is applicable to design and communication problems in virtually any field. For our purposes, the SNR is the ratio of relevant to irrelevant elements or information in a slide or other display. The goal is to have the highest signal-to-noise ratio possible in your slides. People have a hard time coping with excessive cognitive strain. There is simply a limit to a person's ability to process new information efficiently and effectively. Aiming for a higher SNR is an attempt to make things easier for people. Understanding can be hard enough without the excessive and the nonessential bombardment by our visuals that are supposed to be playing a supportive role.

Ensuring the highest possible signal-to-noise ratio means communicating (designing) clearly with as little degradation to the message as possible. Degradation to the visual message can occur in many ways, such as with the selection of inappropriate charts, using ambiguous labels and icons, or unnecessarily emphasizing items such as lines, shapes, symbols, and logos that do not play a key role in support of the message. In other words, if the item can be removed without compromising the visual message, then strong consideration should be given to minimizing the element or removing it altogether. For example, lines in grids or tables can often be made quite thin, lightened, or even removed. And footers and logos, etc. can usually be removed with good results (assuming your company "allows" you to do so).

In *Visual Explanations: Images and Quantities, Evidence and Narrative* (Graphics Press), Edward Tufte refers to an important principle in harmony with SNR called "the smallest effective difference." "Make all visual distinctions as subtle as possible," says Tufte, "but still clear and effective." If the message can be designed with fewer elements, then there is no point in using more.

OPPOSITE PAGE *The slides on the left side are the orginals. The signal-to-noise ratio is improved in the slides on the right by removing nonessential elements and minimizing other elements.*

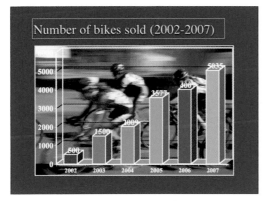

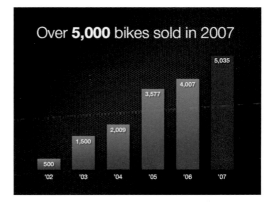

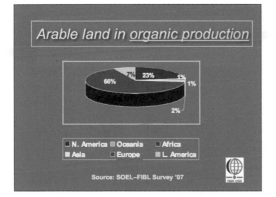

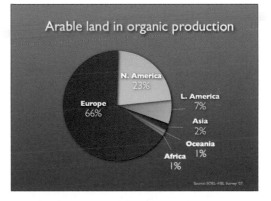

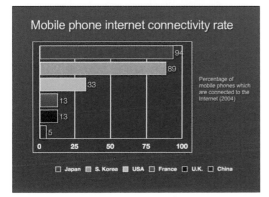

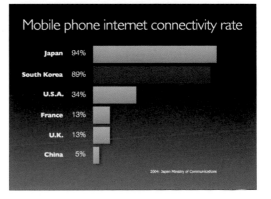

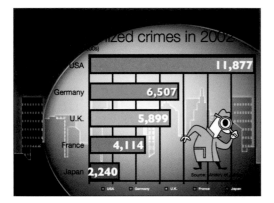

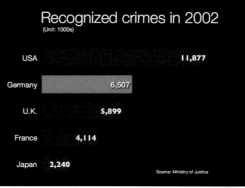

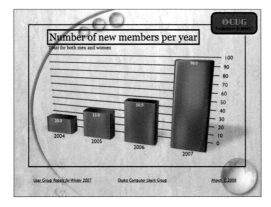

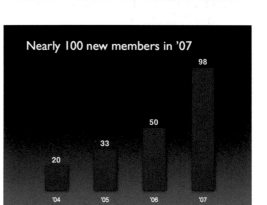

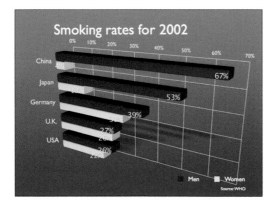

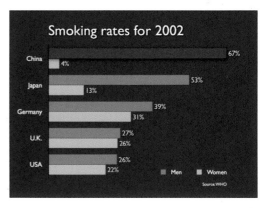

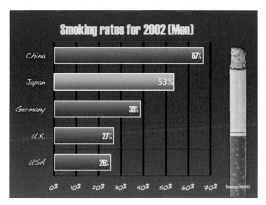

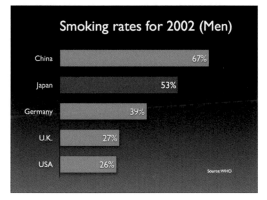

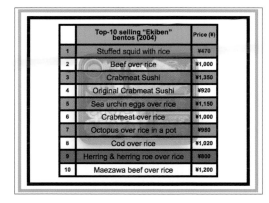

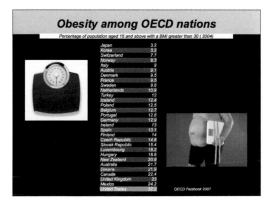

But Is the Nonessential Always "Noise"?

It is generally true that unnecessary elements decrease the design's efficiency and increase the possibility of unintended consequences. But does this mean that we must be uncompromising and remove everything that is not absolutely "essential" to a design? There are those who say a minimalist approach is the most efficient. But efficiency itself is not necessarily an absolute good or always the ideal approach.

When it comes to the display of quantitative information (charts, tables, graphs, etc.), I strongly favor display designs that include the highest SNR possible without any adornment. I use a lot of photographic images in my presentations, so when I do show a chart or a graph, I do not usually place any other elements on the slide. There is nothing wrong with placing a bar chart, for example, over a background image (so long as there is proper contrast or salience), but I think the data itself (with a high SNR) can be a very powerful, memorable graphic on its own.

With other visuals, however, you may want to consider including or retaining elements that serve to support the message at a more emotional level. This may seem like a contradiction with aiming for a high SNR, or the idea that "less is more." However, often emotional elements matter (sometimes a lot). Clarity should be your guiding principle. As with all things, balance is important and the use of emotional elements depends on your particular circumstance, audience, and objectives. In the end, SNR is one principle among many to consider when creating visual messages.

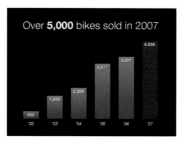

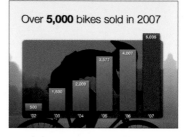

ABOVE *The top slide is simple. The last three slides have "nonessential elements" added that make the slide more interesting, but do not necessarily increase clarity. Any of the designs may be appropriate, however, depending on the situation.*

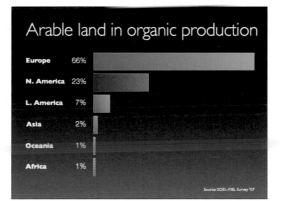

A simple bar chart without the use of an image.

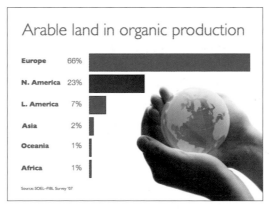

The same simple data with an image added. The image complements the underlining theme —save the planet— without getting in the way of the chart. (Embedded background images on this page and opposite page from iStockphoto.com.)

2-D or Not 2-D? (That Is the Question)

Many of the design tools in Keynote or PowerPoint are quite useful, but the 3-D tool, is one I could do very well without. Taking 2-D data and creating a 3-D chart does not simplify it. The idea is that 3-D may add emotion, but when it comes to charts and graphs, you should aim for simple, clean, and 2-D (for 2-D data). In *The Zen of Creativity* (Ballantine Books), author John Daido Loori, commenting on simplicity, says that the Zen aesthetic "...reflects a simplicity that allows our attention to be drawn to that which is essential, stripping away the extra." What is essential and what is extra is up to you to decide, but stripping away the extra ink that 3-D charts introduce seems like a good place to start. A 3-D representation of 2-D data increases what Edward Tufte calls the "ratio of ink-to-data." While it's nice to have a choice perhaps, 2-D charts and graphs will almost always be a better solution. Three-dimensional charts appear less accurate and can be difficult to comprehend. The viewing angle of the 3-D charts often makes it hard to see where data points sit on an axis. If you do use 3-D charts, avoid extreme perspectives.

The slides below on the left are examples of 3-D effects that compromise the display of very simple data. The slides on the right are possible improvements.

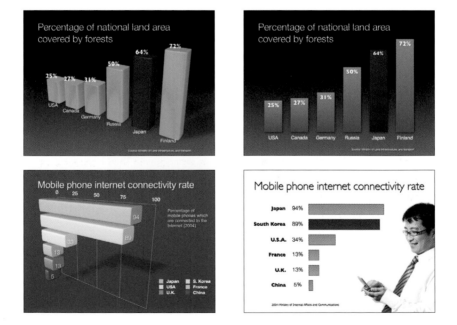

Who Says Your Logo Should Be on Every Slide?

"Branding" is one of the most overused and misunderstood terms in use today. Many people confuse the myriad elements of brand identity with brand or branding. The meaning of brand and branding goes far deeper than simply making one's logo as recognizable as possible. If you are presenting for an organization, try removing logos from all except the first and last slide. If you want people to learn something and remember you, then make a good, honest presentation. The logo won't help make a sell or make a point, but the clutter it brings does add unnecessary noise and makes the presentation visuals look like a commercial. We don't begin every new sentence in a conversation by restating our name, so why should you bombard people with your company logo on every slide?

Most companies with a PowerPoint template certainly insist that their employees use the company logo on every slide. But is this good advice? Slide real estate is limited as it is, so don't clutter it with logos and trademarks, footers, and so on.

Here's some good advice:

"[I]f you want people to understand better, then get that stuff off the screen... Clean it up and get it off because it is simply making it more difficult for people to understand what [you are] saying."

These are the words of Tom Grimes, Kansas State University Journalism professor, speaking about his research on the influence of on-screen clutter on understanding or retention. He's actually talking about the overpowering visual clutter found in TV newscasts, yet his advice is good for our live multimedia presentations as well. Over the past several years, many TV news broadcasts have substituted "pizzazz" and "sizzle"—not to mention conjecture, speculation, and sensationalism—for clean, clear messages. Perhaps the visual clutter found in most TV news broadcasts has spilled over into the corporate slide templates. One thing is for certain: if you want people to hear and understand your visual message, the answer is not to add more clutter but to remove it all.

A Word About Bullet Points

The "traditional way" of doing presentations with slides full of bulleted lists has been going on for so long it is in a sense part of corporate culture. It is simply "the way things are done." Here in Japan, for example, young employees entering the company will be taught, at some point, that when they do presentations with slideware they should put a minimum amount of text in each slide. This sounds like good advice, right? But, a "minimum" means something like six–seven lines of abbreviated text and figures and several complete sentences. The idea of having one or two words (or—gasp!—no words) would be a sign of someone who did not do their homework. A series of text-filled slides with plenty of charts or tables shows that you are a "serious employee." Never mind that the audience can't really see the detail in the slides well (or that the executive board does not really understand your charts). If it looks complicated it must be "good."

I have a shelf full of presentation books in English and Japanese. All of them say "use a minimum of text." Most of them define "minimum" as being anywhere from five to eight lines of bullet points. The "1-7-7 Rule" is advice often given to presenters (proof that conventional wisdom is out of sync). Here's the rub: no one can do a good presentation with slide after slide of bullet points. No one. Bullet points work well when used sparingly in documents to help readers scan content or to summarize key points and so on. But bullet points are usually not effective in a live talk.

The 1-7-7 rule: What is it?

- Have only <u>one</u> main idea per slide
- Insert only <u>seven</u> lines of text maximum.
- Use only <u>seven</u> words per line maximum.
- The question is though: does this work?
- Is this method really good advice?
- Is this really an appropriate, effective "visual"?
- This slide has just seven bullet points!

The presocom company   *"Great slides R easy!"*   *November 15, 2007*

How Many Bullets Points per Slide?

A good general guideline is to use bullet points only very rarely and only after you have considered other options for displaying the information in a way that best supports your point visually. Do not let the default bulleted lists of the software template dictate your decision. Sometimes bullet points may be the best choice. For example, if you are summarizing key specifications of a new product or reviewing the steps in a process, a clear bulleted list may be appropriate depending on your content, objectives, and audience. People will tire quickly, however, if several slides of bulleted lists are shown one after another, so use them with caution. I am not suggesting that you completely abandon the idea of using bullet points in multimedia presentations, but use of bullet points in slides should be a rare exception.

TOP *The blue slide above was my first attempt to summarize the key points from Dan Pink's book* A Whole New Mind *in one slide.*

BOTTOM *The second slide above uses about half the text to summarize the key points in a more engaging, visual way.*

Picture Superiority Effect

The picture superiority effect says that pictures are remembered better than words, especially when people are casually exposed to the information and the exposure is for a very limited time. When information recall is measured just after exposure to a series of pictures or a series of words, the recall for pictures and words is about equal. However, the picture superiority effect applies when the time after exposure is more than 30 seconds, according to research cited in *Universal Principles of Design* (Rockport Publishers). "Use the picture superiority effect to improve the recognition and recall of key information. Use pictures and words together, and ensure that they reinforce the same information for optimal effect," say the authors Lidwell, Holden, and Butler. The effect is strongest when the pictures represent common, concrete things.

You can see the picture superiority effect used widely in marketing communications, such as posters, billboards, brochures, annual reports, etc. The effect should be kept in mind too when designing slides (images and text) that support a narrative. Visual imagery appears to be a powerful mnemonic tool that helps learning and increases retention compared, say, to witnessing someone read words off a screen.

Going Visual

Images are a powerful and natural way for humans to communicate. The key word here is natural. We are hardwired for understanding images and using images to communicate. There seems to be something inside of us—even from a very young age—that yearns to draw or otherwise show the ideas in our head through imagery (drawings, paintings, photography, etc.).

In 2005, Alexis Gerard and Bob Goldstein published *Going Visual: Using Images to Enhance Productivity, Decision-Making and Profits* (Wiley). Gerard and Goldstein urge us to use visuals to tell our story or prove our point. The authors are not talking about using imaging technology because it is "cool" or "modern." Going visual is about using images to improve communication and business. For example, you could write about or talk about how a recent fire impacted production, but wouldn't it be far more powerful to send pictures with a smaller amount of text (or spoken words) to describe the situation? What would be more memorable? Which would have more impact?

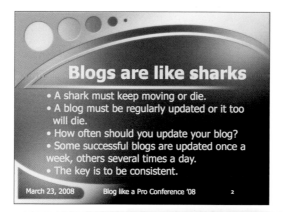

A traditional slide which duplicates the presenter's words. More of a reading test than a visual.

This slide serves to enhance the presenter's spoken words much better. The photo has impact and the point is made clearly. Which slide is more memorable? And since people are not reading, they can actually listen to you. (Photo of shark from iStockphoto.com.)

Using images is an efficient way to compare and contrast changes such as the effects of drought in this simulated example. (The original embedded image of the dry lake bed from iStockphoto.com.)

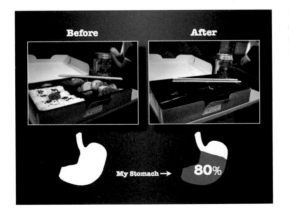

This is a tongue-in-cheek example showing the actual bento I mentioned in Chapter 1 that was the genesis for this book. "Before/after" and "then and now" visual comparisons are easy to create and easy to remember. Al Gore used many "then and now" visual comparisons in his presentations and in the movie Inconvenient Truth to show physical changes over time.

Ask yourself this: What information are you representing with the written word on a slide that you could replace with a photograph (or other appropriate image or graphic)? You still need text for labeling, etc. But if you are using text on a slide for describing something, you probably could use an image instead more effectively.

Images are powerful, efficient, and direct. Images can also be used very effectively as mnemonic devices to make messages more memorable. If people cannot listen and read at the same time, why do most PowerPoint slides contain far more words than images? One reason, historically, is that business people have been limited by technology. Visual communication and technology go hand in hand. In 2008, however, most people do have the basic tools available—for example, digital cameras and editing software—for easily placing photos in slides.

No more excuses. It just takes a different way of looking at presentations. It takes the realization that modern presentations with slides and other multimedia have more in common with cinema (images and narration) and comics (images and text) than they do with written documents. Today's presentations increasingly share more in common with a documentary film than an overhead transparency.

On the following pages you can see a few slides demonstrating different visual treatments in support of a single message. The context is a presentation on gender and labor issues in Japan. The purpose of the slide was to support visually the claim that "72% of the part-time workers in Japan are women." This statistic is from the Japanese Ministry of Labor. The figure "72%" is something the presenter said she wanted the audience to remember as it was discussed again as the presentation progressed. So we designed a slide that was subtle, simple, memorable, and fit into a theme that was appealing and attractive.

This is the original slide. The problem with this slide is that the clip art used does not reinforce the simple statistic, nor does it even fit the theme of women in the Japanese labor market. The background is a tired, overused PowerPoint template, and the text is difficult to read.

The text on this slide is easy to read, and although the clip art is a bit more appropriate for the subject, it still does not give the slide a strong visual impact or overall professional look and feel.

This slide is an effort to display the same information in a pie chart. While this type of chart is not unusual, its 3-D effects and extra lines are not an improvement.

The two bullet points are easy to read in an instant. The photo of an actual part-time female worker in Japan is a step in the right direction, but it could still be much better.

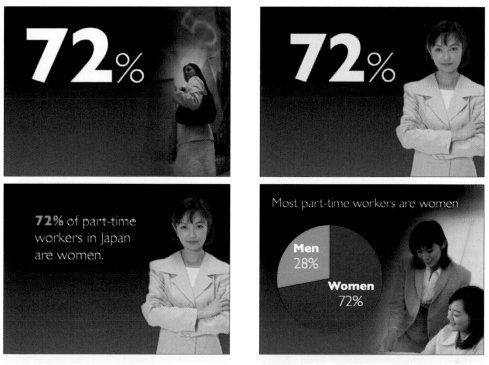

ABOVE *The four slides above are different treatments of the same message. Any of these slides would also work to complement the presenter's narration. (Notice that the slides featuring only the "72%" figure would be virtually meaningless without the presenter's narration.)*

BELOW The slide on the left was the redesign that was used in the end. All the remaining slides in the deck were also redesigned using Japanese stock images giving the entire presentation a consistent visual theme that supported the presenter's words.

All slides on this page use images that "bleed" off the edge, filling the entire screen. Text and image work in harmony. The "masking tape and paper note" is a jpeg image from iStockphoto that provides an interesting effect and prevents the text from getting lost in the background. The masking tape and note element provide good contrast with the text and add depth to the overall visual. The slight angle of the note and text add interest without being distracting.

Slide images on this page from iStockphoto.com.

The slides on this page are from the portfolio of Jeff Brenman, the creator of Apollo Ideas and the winner of SlideShare's "World's Best Presentation Contest" in 2007. (You can see the slide deck that won him first place in the next chapter.) Jeff has a talent for combining images and text in a way that is fresh and effective for augmenting the presenter's messages.

Where Can You Get Good Images?

Getty Images may have the best quality and the greatest selection of images for presentations, but what if you cannot afford to make a slide presentation costing hundreds or thousands of dollars in stock image fees? In this case, low cost, royalty-free "micro-stock" images are an alternative. The site I recommend most often is iStockphoto.com. Most of the images used in this book are from iStockphoto.com. iStockphoto is incredibly easy to use and after you search you can just roll over thumbs to get a larger view without having to open another page.

I do not suggest you limit your image searches to iStockphoto.com only. I have a shelf full of photo CDs and subscribe to other photo sites as well, but iStockphoto is the best. They have over two million images from which to choose and are adding thousands of images every week; they just keep getting better and better. iStockphoto has a "free image of the week" so you may want to check back from time to time to see what's new (and free). At the back of this book, you will find a special code just for you that entitles you to 10 free credits on the iStockphoto Web site (and a discount for current members). So take your free credits and download a few images from iStockphoto.com.

My personal favorite photo site
• iStockphoto (www.istockphoto.com)

Here are some other places to get low-cost images
• Dreams Time (www.dreamstime.com)
• Fotolia (www.fotolia.com)
• Japanese Streets (www.japanesestreets.com)
• Shutter Stock (www.shutterstock.com)
• Shutter Map (www.shuttermap.com)

Here are a few sites that offer free images
• Morgue File (www.morguefile.com)
• Flickr Creative Commons Pool (www.flickr.com/creativecommons)
• Image After (www.imageafter.com)
• Stock.xchng (www.sxc.hu)
• Everystockphoto search engine (www.everystockphoto.com)

Quote This

While long bullet points are not very effective as a "visual enhancer," displaying quotations in your presentation slides can be a very powerful technique. Depending on the presentation, I often use quite a few quotes from various fields to support my points. The trick is not to use them too much and to make sure they are short and legible.

When I first saw Tom Peters live a few years ago while I was working in Silicon Valley, I was happy to see that he used a good deal of quotes from various experts, authors, and industry leaders. Using quotes in his presentation visuals is a big deal for Tom. In fact, it is number 18 on his "Presentation Excellence 56" article on his Web site.

Commenting on why he uses so many PowerPoint slides containing quotes, Tom says:

> "...my conclusions are much more credible when I back them up with Great Sources. I say pretty radical stuff. I say 'Get radical!' That's one thing. But then I show a quote from Jack Welch, who, after all, ran a $150 billion company (I didn't): 'You can't behave in a calm, rational manner; you've got to be out there on the lunatic fringe.' Suddenly my radicalism is "'certified" by a "real operator." Also, I find that people like to get beyond the spoken word, and see a SIMPLE reminder of what I'm saying."

Quotes can indeed add credibility to your story. A simple quote is a good springboard from which you can launch your next topic or weave into your narrative to support your point. Remember, quotes should be short, in most cases, since it can become quite tedious when a presenter reads a paragraph from a screen.

Text within Images

I almost always get my quotes straight from material I have read directly or from personal interviews. My books, for example, are filled with sticky-notes and pages full of my comments and highlighter marks. I sketch a star and write a note to myself next to great passages for future reference. It's kind of messy, but it works for me when I put the presentation together later.

When I use a quote I sometimes use a graphic element that targets people's emotions, ads more visual interest, and enhances the effect of the slide. But rather than using a small photo or other element, consider placing the text within a larger photo. To do this you will want to use an image at least as large as your slide dimensions (e.g., 800x600) for your background. Look for an image that supports the point you are making with the quotation. The image should have plenty of empty space so that your text can fit comfortably in the slide with good contrast.

On this page you can see two slides displaying a quotation in a manner that is not unusual. On the opposite page you can see the same quote displayed *within* the image rather than simply next to a smaller version of the image in a slide. *(Photos in these slides from iStockphoto.com.)*

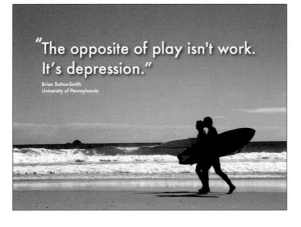

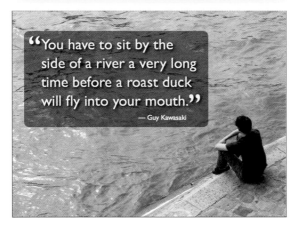

Emptiness which is conceptually liable to be mistaken for sheer nothingness is in fact the reservoir of infinite possibilities.

— Daisetz Suzuki

Empty Space

Empty space (also called negative space or white space) is a concept that is supremely simple, yet the most difficult for people to apply. Whether people are designing a document or a slide, the urge to fill empty areas with more elements is just too great. One of the biggest mistakes that typical business people make with presentation slides (and documents as well) is going out of their way to seemingly use every centimeter of space on a page, filling it up with text, boxes, clip art, charts, footers, and the ubiquitous company logo.

Empty space implies elegance and clarity. This is true with graphic design, but you can see the importance of space (both visual and physical) in the context of, say, interior design as well. High-end brand shops are always designed to create as much open space as possible. Empty space can convey a feeling of high quality, sophistication, and importance.

Empty space has a purpose. But those new to design may only see the positive elements, such as text or a graphic, without ever "seeing" the empty space and using that space to make the design more compelling. It is the empty space that gives a design air and lets the positive elements breathe. If it were true that empty space in a design such as a slide were "wasted space," then it would make sense to want to remove such waste. However, empty space in a design is not "nothing," it is indeed a powerful "something," which gives the few elements on your slide their power.

In the Zen arts, you will find an appreciation for empty space. A painting, for example, may be mostly "empty" except for two to three elements, but the placement of the elements within that space forms a powerful message. The same approach can be applied to a room. Many Japanese homes have a washitsu, a traditional room with tatami mats, which is simple and mostly empty. The empty space allows for the appreciation of a single item, such as a single flower or a single wall hanging. The emptiness is a powerful design element itself. In this case, the more we add, the more diluted and less effective the design of our graphic, or living space, becomes.

Using Empty Space

The blue slide on top is a typical one with several bullet points and an image related to the topic. Rather than making good use of empty space, the blue slide has trapped space in areas around the image. Instead of using one busy slide, I broke the flow of the content into six slides for the introduction of the "Hara hachi bu" concept. Since it is not necessary to put all the words that are spoken by the presenter on the screen, much of the on-screen text was removed. The slides have a clean white background with plenty of active empty space that helps guide the viewer's eyes. When a new slide is revealed the eye will be naturally drawn to the image first (it's larger, colorful) and then quickly go to the text element.

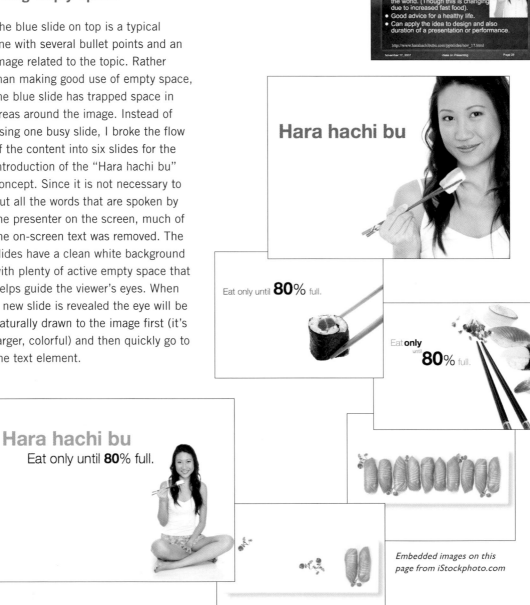

Embedded images on this page from iStockphoto.com

Directing the Eye With Images

Images can be used to help guide your viewer's eyes through a slide to the most important elements. If you use images of people, be careful not to have these images unintentionally guide your viewer's eyes away from what you want them to see. For example, if the text element (or chart) is the highest priority, it is important not to have images of people looking in the opposite direction from those elements. How do the images in these slides guide your eyes toward or away from the other elements? Which versions of the slides on this page look more harmonious?

Balance

Balance in a design is important, and one way to achieve good balance and clarity with a design is through the intelligent use of "empty space." A well-balanced design has a clear, single, unified message. A well-designed slide has a clear starting point and guides the viewer through the design. The viewer should never have to "think" about where to look. A visual must never confuse anyone. What is the most important, less important, and least important parts of the design can be clearly expressed by having a clear hierarchy and a good balance of the display elements.

Empty space can be dynamic and active through careful placement of positive elements. Conscious use of empty space can even bring motion to your design. In this way, the empty space is not passive but active. If you want to bring a more dynamic feel and interest to your slide design, then consider using an asymmetrical design. Asymmetrical designs activate empty space and make your design more interesting. Asymmetrical designs are more informal and are dynamic, with a variety of sizes and shapes.

Symmetrical designs have a strong emphasis along a central vertical axis. Symmetrical balance is vertically centered and is equivalent on both sides. Symmetrical designs are more static than asymmetrical designs and evoke feelings of formality or stability. There is nothing wrong with centered, symmetrical designs, although empty space in such designs is generally passive and pushed to the side.

Design is about seeing and manipulating shapes, but if we do not see the empty space in a slide as a shape, then it will be ignored and any use of empty space will be accidental. Consequently, the results will not be as powerful. Good presentations will incorporate a series of presentation visuals that have a mix of slides that are symmetrical and asymmetrical.

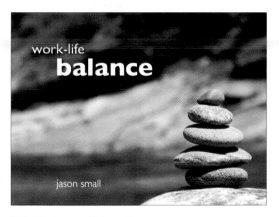

Both slides have good balance. The top slide is a common design that is symmetrical (and not very interesting). The bottom slide is asymmetrical and is simpler yet more powerful as a visual. (Image from iStockphoto.com.)

One way to activate the empty space and create a dynamic, asymmetrical slide is to use large images that "bleed" off the edge. Use the empty space to place small amounts of text or other elements. On the right is another Guy Kawasaki quote—one of my favorites—from one of my branding talks in Japan. The first slide (the quote) is symmetrical. The other two slides are examples of asymmetrical designs.

*Embedded images above
from iStockphoto.com*

Grids and the Rule of Thirds

For centuries, artists and designers have introduced a proportion called the "golden mean" or "golden ratio" found in nature into their works. The golden section rectangle has a proportion of 1:1.618. There is a belief that we are naturally drawn to images that have proportions approaching the golden section rectangle, just as we are often drawn to many things in the natural environment with golden-mean proportions. However, attempting to design visuals according to golden-mean proportions is impractical in most cases. But, the "rule of thirds," which is derived from the golden mean, is a basic design technique that can help you add balance (symmetrical or asymmetrical), beauty, and a higher aesthetic quality to your visuals.

The rule of thirds is a basic technique that photographers learn for framing their shots. Subjects placed exactly in the middle can often make for an uninteresting photo. A viewfinder can be divided by lines—real or just imagined—so that you have four intersecting lines or crossing points and nine boxes that resemble a tic-tac-toe board. These four crossing points (also called "power points," if you can believe it) are areas you might place your main subject, rather than in the center.

Remember, there is no liberty in "absolute freedom" when it comes to design. You need to limit your choices so that you do not waste time adjusting every single design element to a new position. I recommend that you create some sort of clean, simple grid to build your visuals upon. Although you may not be aware of it, virtually every Web page and every page in a book or magazine is built atop a grid. Grids can save you time and ensure that your design elements fit more harmoniously on the display. Using grids to divide your slide "canvas" into thirds, for example, is an easier way to at least approach golden-mean proportions, and you can use the grids to align elements that give the overall design balance, a clear flow and point of focus, and a natural overall cohesiveness and aesthetic quality that is not accidental but is by design.

On this page you can see five samples of simple slides in which elements were arranged with the help of the "rule of thirds" grid (you can easily create your own using the guides in Keynote or PowerPoint). The rule of thirds is not a rule at all, it is only a guideline. But it is a very useful guideline to use when you are aiming to achieve a balanced look.

You'll also notice that the images themselves have pretty good "rule of third" proportions. The iStockphoto images were chosen in part based on the photo's proportions and how the image guided the eye and contained empty space for text or other design elements. (Images used for the slides on this page are from iStockphoto.com.)

The Big Four: Contrast, Repetition, Alignment, Proximity

These four principles are not all there is to know about graphic design, but understanding these simple related concepts and applying them to slide design can make for far more satisfying and effective designs.

Contrast

Contrast simply means difference. And for whatever reason—perhaps our brains think they are still back in the savannah scanning for wild predators—we are all wired to notice differences. We are not conscious of it, but we are scanning and looking for similarities and differences all the time. Contrast is what we notice, and it's what gives a design its energy. So you should make elements that are not the same clearly different, not just slightly different.

Contrast is one of the most powerful design concepts of them all because really any design element can be contrasted with another. You can achieve contrast in many ways—for example, through the manipulation of space (near and far, empty and filled), through color choices (dark and light, cool and warm), by text selection (serif and sans serif, bold and narrow), by positioning of elements (top and bottom, isolated and grouped), and so on.

Making use of contrast can help you create a design in which one item is clearly dominant. This helps the viewer "get" the point of your design quickly. Every good design has a strong and clear focal point and having a clear contrast among elements (with one being clearly dominant) helps. If all items in a design are of equal or similar weight with weak contrast and with nothing being clearly dominant, it is difficult for the viewer to know where to begin. Designs  with strong contrast attract interest, and help the viewer make sense of the visual. Weak contrast is not only boring, but it can be confusing.

Every single element of a design such as line, shape, color, texture, size, space, type, and so on can be manipulated to create contrast. On the next page are some slides that make good use of contrast compared with slides that have weaker contrast.

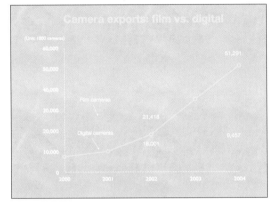

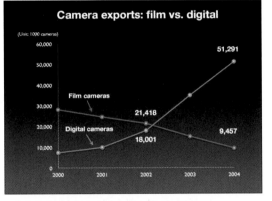

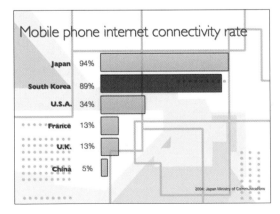

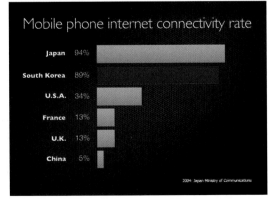

Repetition

The principle of repetition simply means the reusing of the same or similar elements throughout your design. Repetition of certain design elements in a slide or among a deck of slides will bring a clear sense of unity, consistency, and cohesiveness. Where contrast is about showing differences, repetition is about subtly using elements to make sure the design is viewed as being part of a larger whole. If you use a stock template from your software application, then repetition is already built into your slides. For example, a consistent background and consistent use of type adds unity across a deck of slides.

However, you must be careful not to have too much repetition among your slides. Most of the built-in templates have been seen many times before and may not suit your unique situation. Many of the standard templates also have background elements that will soon become tiring, rather than generating interest the tenth time a different slide is shown but with the same repetitive element. For example, a starfish in the lower right (not my favorite but perhaps appropriate for a presentation on marine biology) is an element that would be a stronger repetitive element if its size and location occasionally shifted in harmony with the content of different slides and in a way that was subtle and did not interfere with the primary message.

The slides on the next page are a good example of repetition. In these slides from a presentation on the process of designing a book, Swiss designer and photographer Markuz Wernli Saito used his own full bleed photos for all his slides. To help give the entire presentation a unified look, he used a similar red note and paperclip to "hold" his text in each slide. The placement of the note and paperclip image was not always in the same location in every slide, nor was the size always the same, but the consistent use of this one element and the red color served to ad a subtle repetitive element that gave his visuals a professional and unified look.

Alignment

The whole point of the alignment principle is that nothing in your slide design should look as if it were placed there randomly. Every element is connected visually via an invisible line. Where repetition is more concerned with elements across a deck of slides, alignment is about obtaining unity among elements of a single slide. Even elements that are quite far apart on a slide should have a visual connection, something that is easier to achieve with the use of grids. When you place elements on a slide, try to align them with another element.

Many people fail to make an effort to apply the alignment principle, which often results in elements being almost aligned but not quite. This may not seem like a big deal, but these kinds of slides look less sophisticated and overall less professional. The audience may not be conscious of it, but slides that contain elements in alignment look cleaner. And assuming other principles are applied harmoniously as well, your slides should be easier to understand quickly.

Proximity

The principle of proximity is about moving things closer or farther apart to achieve a more organized look. The principle says that related items should be grouped together so that they will be viewed as a group, rather than as several unrelated elements. Audiences will assume that items that are not near each other in a design are not closely related. Audiences will naturally tend to group similar items that are near to each other into a single unit.

People should never have to "work" at trying to figure out which caption goes with which graphic or whether or not a line of text is a subtitle or a line of text unrelated to the title. Do not make audiences think. That is, do not make them "think" about the wrong stuff, like trying to decipher your slide's organization and design priority. A slide is not a page in a book or magazine, so you are not going to have more than a few elements or groups of elements. Robin Williams, in her best-selling book *The Non-Designer's Design Book* (Peachpit Press) says that we must be conscious of where our eye goes first when we step back and look at our design. When you look at your slide, notice where your eye is drawn first, second, and so on. What path does your eye take?

This title slide lacks a design priority. Due to poor use of alignment and proximity the slide seems to contain five different elements.

Principles of Presentation Design:

Tips on how to think like a designer

By Less Nessman

Director of the PRKW Institute

This slide uses symmetrical balance and better proximity, with related items now clearly together. Greater contrast is also achieved by adjusting type size and color to give the design a clear priority.

The two slides on this page show that by aligning all elements flush right, a strong invisible line is created on the right side that ties all elements together in a way that is more interesting than the more common symmetrical title. Type and color are adjusted to create greater contrast and interest. The red dot in the title ties in with the red logo at the bottom.

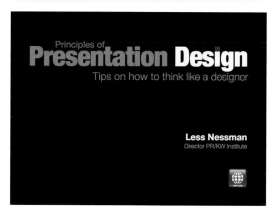

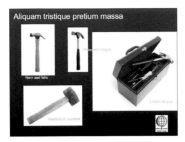

The slide on the left looks busier due to the abrupt contrast between the background color of the images. By aligning the text and the photos and making the image backgrounds transparent (in this case by simply changing the slide background to white) the slide is much cleaner and "noise" is reduced.

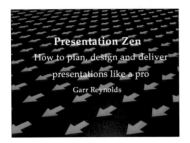
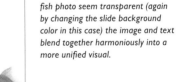

The background image on the slide on the left has too much salience, making the title hard to see. Choosing a more appropriate background image that allows the text to remain clearly in the foreground and grouping the text lines makes for a stronger title slide.

By making the background of the fish photo seem transparent (again by changing the slide background color in this case) the image and text blend together harmoniously into a more unified visual.

The slide on the left has a busy template which makes the useful area of the slide about 1/3 smaller. The slide on the right uses the image to cover the entire slide. The text is clearly foreground and the image serves both as background and at times foreground, making the overall visual more dynamic and more unified with a cleaner, more dramatic look.

Images on this page and opposite page from iStockphoto.com.

This slide features a typical graph exported from Excel. It is impossible to identify the countries as the text is too small and at an angle. The biggest problem is this is too much data for a display. This amount of information would be better presented in a handout.

The text and data are easier to see as the contrast between the foreground and background is much better. Only the key variables are chosen to include in the display, which allows the bars and figures to be larger. Information on the excluded variables can be put into a document to be taken away.

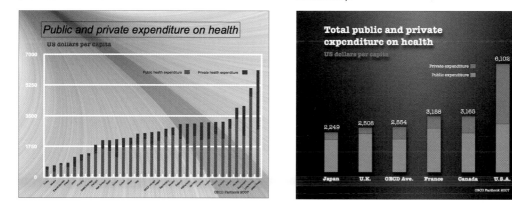

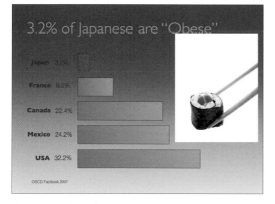

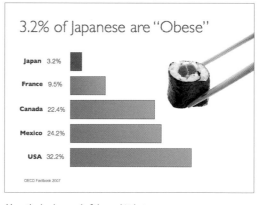

The background color is not a good fit with the colors of the bars nor does it provide enough contrast; the text is hard to read. The background of the sushi photo adds unnecessary noise to the visual.

Here the background of the sushi photo "disappears" to match the white background of the slide. The text and bars and background have much better contrast and are easier to read.

The more strikingly visual your presentation is, the more people will remember it. And more importantly, they will remember you.

— Paul Arden

In Sum

- Design matters. But design is not about decoration or about ornamentation. Design is about making communication as easy and clear for the viewer as possible.

- Keep the principle of signal-versus-noise in mind to remove all nonessential elements. Remove visual clutter. Avoid 3-D effects.

- People remember visuals better than bullet points. Always ask yourself how you can use a strong visual—including quantitative displays—to enhance your narrative.

- Empty space is not nothing; it is a powerful something. Learn to see and manipulate empty space to give your slide designs greater organization, clarity, and interest.

- Use the principle of contrast to create strong dynamic differences among elements that are different. If it is different, make it *very* different.

- Use the principle of repetition to repeat selected elements throughout your slides. This can help give your slides unity and organization.

- Use the principle of alignment to connect elements visually (through invisible lines) on a slide. Grids are very useful for achieving good alignment. This will give your slide a clean, well-organized look.

- Use the principle of proximity to ensure that related items are grouped together. People will tend to interpret items together or near to each other as belonging to the same group.

Sample Slides: Images & Text

In this chapter you can review slides from several different presenters who make presentations often in "the real world." (Because of limited space, only a small number of slides are shown from each presentation.) Not all of the sample slides are necessarily perfect. However, while we can judge a slide in terms of its adherence to basic design principles, it is difficult to judge the effectiveness of a slide design without seeing how the visuals are used in a live talk.

Though the content and circumstances are different in each case, what the slides in this chapter have in common is that they are simple, highly visual, and served (or could serve) a successful supportive role in a live talk, augmenting the presenter's narrative and helping to make things clear.

Your slides should be engaging and "part of the show," but they must also be easy to understand quickly. If you need to explain something quite complex, then build (animate) the parts of your chart or diagram in steps in a way that is logical and clear. Simplicity, restraint, and harmony are important considerations when designing slides or other multimedia. The goal is not to make slides "look good." The goal is clarity. However, if you design slides while always mindful of the principles of simplicity and restraint—as well as the basic design concepts outlined in Chapter 6—your slides will indeed look attractive.

Differentiation

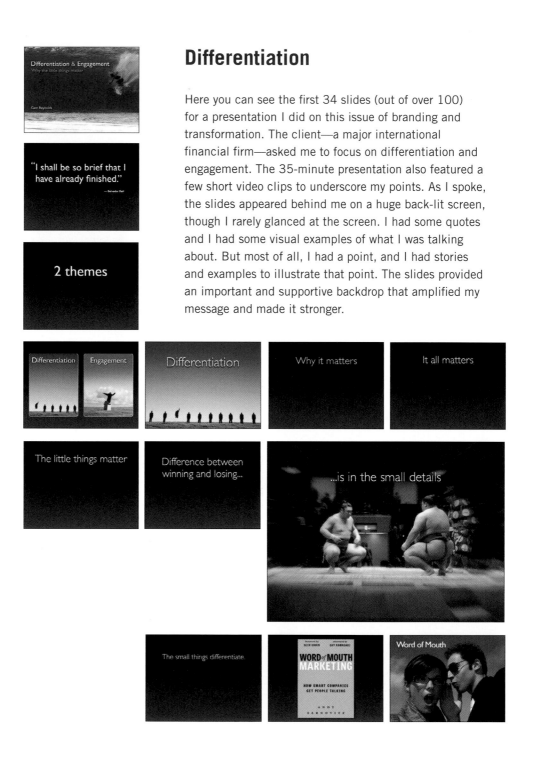

Here you can see the first 34 slides (out of over 100) for a presentation I did on this issue of branding and transformation. The client—a major international financial firm—asked me to focus on differentiation and engagement. The 35-minute presentation also featured a few short video clips to underscore my points. As I spoke, the slides appeared behind me on a huge back-lit screen, though I rarely glanced at the screen. I had some quotes and I had some visual examples of what I was talking about. But most of all, I had a point, and I had stories and examples to illustrate that point. The slides provided an important and supportive backdrop that amplified my message and made it stronger.

Shift Happens*

Jeff Brenman
Founder and CEO, Apollo Ideas
www.apolloideas.com

The slides in this presentation feature a stylization
of a slideshow originally created by Karl Fisch,
examining globalization and America's future in
the 21st century. It's designed for on-line viewing.
However, in a live talk some of the text could be
removed, making the slides a better complement to
the speaker's words. You can find all the slides used
in this presentation on Slideshare.net:

www.slideshare.net/jbrenman

An official update to the original Shift Happens video
presentation from Karl Fisch and Scott McLeod can
be seen on Wikispaces.com:

www.shifthappens.wikispaces.com

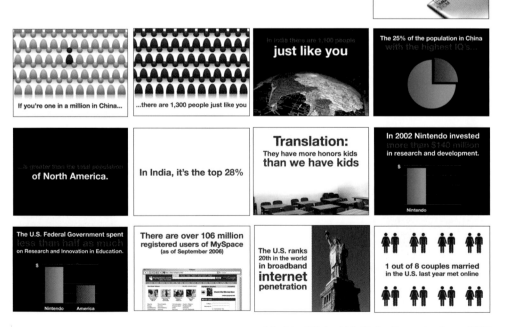

* 1st Prize, Slideshare's World's Best Presentation Contest (2007).

If you took every single job in the U.S. today **and shipped it to China...**

During the course of this presentation...

60 babies
will be born in the U.S.

244 babies
will be born in China

351 babies
will be born in India

The U.S. Department of Labor estimates that today's learner will have 10–14 jobs ...by the age of

38

1 out of 4 workers today
is working for a company they have been employed by for less than one year

more than 1 out of 2
are working for a company they have worked for for less than five years.

According to former Secretary of Education **Richard Riley...**

...the top 10 in-demand jobs in 2010 **did not exist in 2004**

We are currently preparing students **for jobs that** don't yet exist...

using technologies **that haven't** been invented...

in order to solve problems we don't even know are problems yet.

POP QUIZ
Name this country...

✓ Richest in the world
✓ Largest military
✓ Center of world business and finance
✓ Strongest education system
✓ World center of innovation and invention
✓ Currency the world standard of value
✓ Highest standard of living

England... in 1900

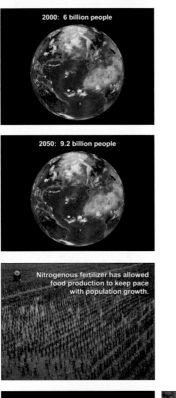

The Sustainable Food Lab*

Chris Landry
Director of Development & Communications
Sustainable Food Laboratory
www.sustainablefoodlab.org

The slides here are part of a modified slide deck Chris Landry uses for talks about his organization and the work they do to bring more sustainability to mainstream food systems. Chris added a bit more copy to these slides so they will make a little more sense when viewed without narration in printed form, but the visuals were originally created to augment his live talk. You can find all the slides used in this presentation on Slideshare.net:

www.slideshare.net/chrislandry

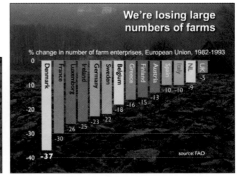

* 3rd Prize, Slideshare's World's Best Presentation Contest (2007).

Truemors

Guy Kawasaki

Co-founder of Truemors

www.truemors.com

The slides here were used by Guy Kawasaki in a presentation entitled How I Launched a Web 2.0, User-Generated Content, Citizen Journalism, Long-Tail, Social Media Site for only $10,918.09 (which may be the world's longest title for a pitch). In his own charismatic way Guy revealed a number and then elaborated on the meaning of the figure. The slides are not meant to stand alone though you can get the gist of his main points from the slides. In the live talk the simplicity of the slides was a good complement to the spoken word. You can find all the slides used in this presentation on Slideshare.net:

www.slideshare.net/GKawasaki

The slides were created by Scott Schwertly of Ethos3 Communications (www.ethos3.com).

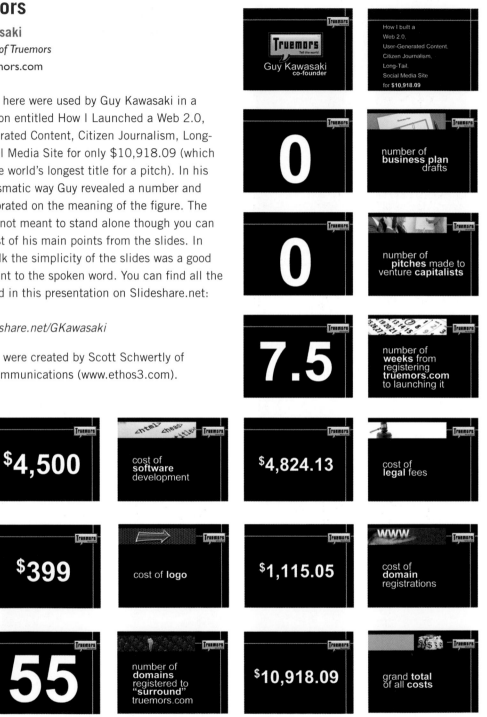

My Declaration
of Independence

Pam Slim

Speaker, coach, business consultant

www.escapefromcubiclenation.com

The few slides here are from a longer presentation called
My Declaration of Independence that Pam Slim and her team
designed to be used in live presentations and also for an
inspirational piece done in Flash and set to music available
on her Web site. For the live talk, Pam can remove more of
the text so that the slides complement her words.

You can watch the Flash version of this presentation on Pam's
corporate site, Ganas Consulting:

www.ganas.com

Aromatic Chemistry

Dr. Aisyah Saad Abdul Rahim

Lecturer in Pharmaceutical Chemistry
School of Pharmaceutical Sciences
Universiti Sains Malaysia.

www.pha.usm.my/pharmacy/Aisyah2006.htm

The visuals here are typical of the lecture slides now used by Dr. Saad in her Pharmaceutical Chemistry classes in Malaysia. These are samples of her lecture slides on "Aromatic Chemistry." The black and red slides serve as a historical introduction to benzene, whereas the second group of slides illustrate the four essential features of aromatic compounds.

"I teach 'Aromatic Chemistry' to pharmacy students," says Dr. Saad. "Mindful of Asian students' penchant towards rote learning, I decided to apply the Presentation Zen approach in my lectures. The first few lectures had the students baffled because they could hardly jot down any notes. Later, they figured out that they had to pay more attention to my lectures. I use the Presentation Zen approach because it appeals to me visually and provides an amazing way to make students listen and understand more in lectures rather than just copying down notes off my slides."

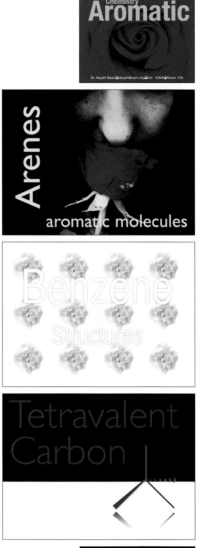

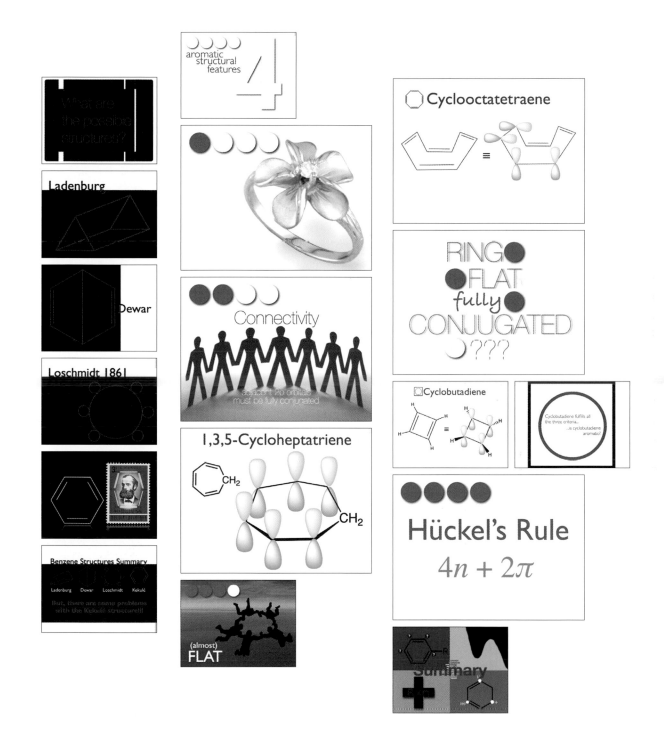

Presenting on Animal-Based Issues

Sangeeta Kumar, M.Ed.
Education Coordinator
People for the Ethical Treatment of Animals
www.peta.org

In her position as Education Coordinator for People for the Ethical Treatment of Animals, Sangeeta travels a lot giving highly visual presentations on animal-based issues. The sample slides on this page are from a presentation called Animal Rights and Wrongs. The slides on the opposite page are from her talk called Vegetarian is the New Prius.

"When dealing with a complex or controversial issue, it is important to communicate your ideas in a way that the audience can relate to and visualize," Sangeeta says. "In these examples, rather than relying on bar graphs or heady quotes, I use engaging photographs and easy to understand facts to help the audience visualize how their food choices impact animals and the environment."

See more designs by Sangeeta on her corporate Web site:

www.kumaridesigns.com

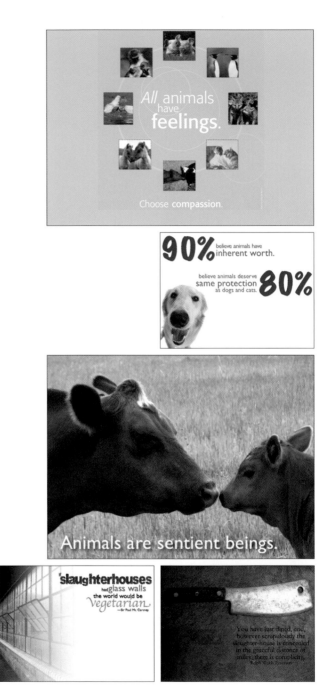

Vegetarian Is The New Prius | Meat Eating and the Environment

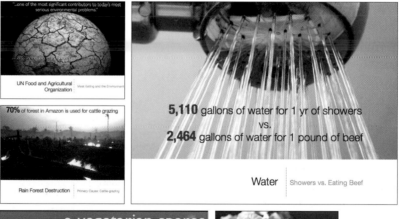

Inbox Zero

Merlin Mann

Productivity guru and creator of 43 folders

www.43folders.com

www.merlinmann.com

The slides here are just some of the ones used by Merlin Mann in a talk he gave in the summer of 2007 at Google for their Tech Talk series. The presentation was about strategies for dealing with high-volume email and the importance of getting your inbox to zero. These simple slides—created with images from iStockphoto.com—served as a good supportive backdrop as he told his story. You can find a video of Merlin's "Inbox Zero" presentation on YouTube and Google Video.

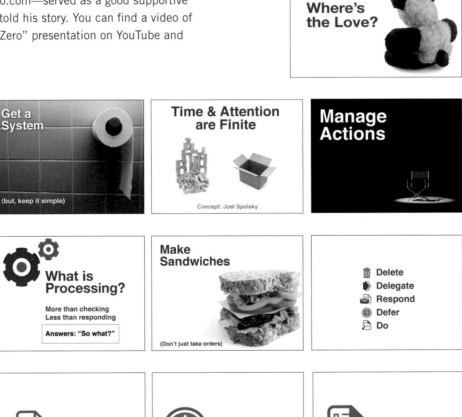

In Sum

A good visual will enhance the speaker's message. The slides featured here are a very small sample that highlight what's possible when you combine images and text. From a technical point of view, these slides were not too difficult to produce. All that was needed was PowerPoint or Keynote, and image editing software such as Adobe Photoshop Elements. What you design your slides or other visuals to look like depends completely on your unique situation and your audience, but keep the following in mind:

• Create visuals that are simple with clear design priorities that contain elements which guide the viewer's eye.

• Have a visual theme but avoid tired, overused software templates.

• Limit bullet points or avoid them completely.

• Use high quality graphics.

• Build (animate) complex graphics to support your narrative.

• Think "maximum effect with minimum means."

• Learn to see empty space, and learn to use it in a way that brings greater clarity to visuals.

delivery

Be here now. Be someplace else later. Is that so complicated?

— David Bader

The Art of Being Completely Present

We are offended when we try to have a conversation or a meeting with someone who seems preoccupied, who is not fully "there," listening and contributing. Yet we have become quite accustomed to enduring speakers and presenters who are not fully engaged with the audience and with the topic. One of the most important things to remember when delivering a presentation is to be fully present at that moment in time. A good presenter is fully committed to the moment, committed to being there with the audience at that particular place and time. He may have pressing problems—who doesn't?—but he puts those aside so that he may be fully "there." When you give a presentation, your mind should not be filled and racing with a million concerns, distracted from the here and now. It is impossible to have a real conversation with someone when he is "somewhere else." Likewise, it is impossible to have a truly successful presentation when you are "somewhere else."

One of the most fundamental things you can learn from the world of Zen is the art of mindfulness. You may know of mindfulness in its association with meditation (zazen). But the interesting thing about Zen is that it is not separate from the real world. That is, Zen makes no distinction between ordinary life and "religious life." Meditation is not an escape from reality at all, and in fact even everyday routines can be methods for meditation. When you have an awareness that your actions and judgments are usually just automatic reactions based on a sort of running dialogue that you have in your head, then you are free to let go of such judgments. So, rather than hating washing the dishes, you just wash the dishes. When you write a letter, you write a letter. And when you give a presentation, you give a presentation.

Mindfulness is concerned with the here and now and having an awareness of this particular moment. You want to see this moment as it is without your ordinary filters, filters that are concerned only with the past (or future) and of how things should or will be and so on. True mindfulness is accessible to all, though it is not easy to obtain. Our lives are so crazy these days doing email, sending text messages, surfing the Web, or driving late in rush hour traffic to pick up the kids while ordering dinner on a mobile phone. There are so many things on our minds and so many worries. Worries are the worst things of all because they are always about the past or about the future, two things that do not even exist in the present. In our daily lives and in our work lives, including presenting, we've got to clear our minds and be only one place: right here.

Photo credit: Macworld.com

Steve Jobs and the Art of the Swordsman

Much has been written about the approach to presentations taken by Steve Jobs. His slides, for example, are always simple, stunning, and highly visual, and he uses them smoothly and seamlessly, advancing all slides and effects by himself without ever drawing attention to the fact that he is the one advancing the slides. His style is conversational, and his visuals are in perfect sync with his words. His presentations are built on a solid structure, which gives them an easy feeling of flow as if he were taking us on a small journey. He is friendly, comfortable, and confident (which make others feel relaxed), and he exudes a level of passion and enthusiasm that is engaging without going over the top.

It all seems so automatic and natural. It all seems so easy, so you'd be tempted to think that it just comes naturally to Steve, and that it's a pretty easy task for him to use his natural charisma to woo a crowd. But you'd be wrong. While it is true that Steve Jobs is a charismatic figure, I'm not sure giving presentations with multimedia support, and even giving live demos (how many CEOs do that?), is something that comes naturally to anyone. No, the reason Steve Jobs's presentations go so well and are so engaging is because he and his team prepare and practice like mad to make sure it looks "easy."

When Steve is on stage he is, in a sense, an artist. And like any artist, through practice and experience, he has perfected his technique and form. Yet, also like the trained artist, there is no thought of technique or of form, or even of failure or success while performing the art. Once we think of failure or success, we are like the swordsman whose mind stops, ever so briefly, to ponder his technique or the outcome of the fight. The moment he does, he has lost. This sounds paradoxical, but once we allow our mind to drift to thoughts of success and failure or of outcomes and technique while performing our art, we have at that moment begun our descent.

To see free videos of recent presentations by Steve Jobs go to the Apple Special Events section on the Apple Web site:

www.apple.com/quicktime/guide/appleevents

The Mind That Is No Mind

When a swordsman is in the moment and his mind is empty (*mushin no shin* or the "mind that is no mind"), there are no emotions stemming from fear, there are no thoughts of winning or of losing or even of using the sword. In this way, says Daisetz Suzuki in *Zen and Japanese Culture* (Princeton University Press), "both man and sword turn into instruments in the hands of the unconscious, and it is the unconscious that achieves wonders of creativity. It is here that swordplay becomes an art."

Beyond mastering technique, the secret to swordsmanship rests in obtaining a proper mental state of "no mind" where the mind is "abandoned and yet not abandoned." Frankly, if you are engaged in any art or even a sports match (think Tiger Woods), you must get rid of the obtruding self-consciousness or ego-consciousness and apply yourself completely, but also, as Suzuki says, "...as if nothing particular were taking place at the moment." When you perform in a state of "no mind," you are free from the burdens of inhibitions and doubt and can contribute fully and fluidly in the moment. Artists know this state of mind, as do musicians and highly trained athletes.

These highly anticipated presentations that Steve Jobs does come with a lot of pressure to get it right. A lot is riding on each presentation and expectations are high inside and outside Apple. Yet what makes Steve so effective in these situations is that he is able to seemingly forget the seriousness of the situation and just "perform." In this way, he is like the artful swordsman who through his "immovable mind" has no thought of life or death. The mind has been quieted, and the man is free to be fully present. As Suzuki puts it: "The waters are in motion all the time, but the moon retains its serenity. The mind moves in response to ten thousand situations but remains ever the same."

Technical training is important, but technical training is something acquired and will always have the feel of artificiality unless one has the proper state of mind. "Unless the mind which avails itself of the technical skill somehow attunes itself to a state of the utmost fluidity or mobility," says Suzuki, "anything acquired or superimposed lacks spontaneity of natural growth." In this sense, I think instructors and books can help us become better at presenting well, but ultimately, like many other performance arts, it must grow within us.

You need technique and proper form, and you need to know "the rules." You must practice and then practice some more. When you put in the hard work in the preparation phase and internalize the material, you can perform your art—the art of presentation—in a way that is more natural by obtaining the proper state of mind, that is, "no mind."

Lost in the Moment

Have you ever been lost in the moment while presenting or performing? I do not mean lost as in losing your place. I mean being so in the moment—without worry of the past or future—that you are as demonstrably interested in your topic as your audience has become. This is a true connection.

In *If You Want to Write*, Brenda Ueland speaks of the importance of being in the moment to maximize your creativity and impact on an audience. The harnessing of this creative energy and being fully present is more of an intuitive activity, not an intellectual one. Ueland compares this kind of creativity and connection to a wonderful musical performance.

In playing a musical instrument such as the piano, for example, sometimes you play at it and sometimes you play in it. The goal is not to repeat the notes on a page but to play beautiful music. To be *in it*, not separate from it. Great musicians play in it (even if they are not always technically perfect). The same thing holds for presentations. The aim should be to be in it completely at that moment in time. Perfection of technique is not obtainable perhaps (or even desirable), but a kind of perfect connection can exist between the audience and artist (or presenter) when she "plays in it."

"Only when you play in a thing," Ueland says, "do people listen and hear you and are moved." Your music is believable and authentic because you are "lost in it," not intellectualizing it or following a set of prescribed rules (notes, instructions). We are moved because the artist is clearly and authentically moved as well. Can this not hold true for presentations? Your presentation is believable because you are prepared and logical, but also because you too are moved by your topic. You have to believe in your message completely or no one else will. You must believe in your story fully and be "lost in the moment" of engaging your audience.

"The waters are in motion all the time, but the moon retains its serenity. The mind moves in response to ten thousand situations but remains ever the same."

—Daisetz Suzuki

Learning from the Art of Judo

The best presentation advice can be found in unusual places. Consider the following five principles, for example. These precepts offer good advice for delivering effective presentations:

> (1) Carefully observe oneself and one's situation, carefully observe others, and carefully observe one's environment.
> (2) Seize the initiative in whatever you undertake.
> (3) Consider fully, act decisively.
> (4) Know when to stop.
> (5) Keep to the middle.

These are wise words indeed, but these are not "effective presentation principles" at all, they are Jigoro Kano's Five Principles of Judo as outlined by John Stevens in *Budo Secrets* (Shambhala; New Ed edition). Yet, it is easy to see how these principles can be applied in your efforts to design and deliver presentations. For example, you may have witnessed a presentation where the speaker could have done much better if he had only embraced the wisdom of principle number (4)—know when to stop. There are times when you may speak longer or shorter than planned, but it must be a conscious decision based on the context of the moment and made by following principle number (1)—observing oneself and the situation, observing others and the environment. This is just one small example illustrating the application of such principles.

Jigoro Kano founded judo in the late 1800s, and although judo is not based on the principles of Zen outright, judo is seen by many to be a great expression of Zen concepts. I have a mountain of respect for people who dedicate themselves to the art of judo. Judo is more than a sport or a mere physical activity born in Japan. To those who practice it, the lessons, wisdom, and experience gained serve to help them in profound ways in all aspects of life.

Commenting on the secrets of Judo, H. Seichiro Okazaki said: "Only by cultivating a receptive state of mind, without preconceived ideas or thoughts, can one master the secret art of reacting spontaneously and naturally without hesitation and without purposeless resistance."

This idea need not be confined to the mat. Think about the last challenging presentation you had that just did not go as well as you had hoped. Perhaps there was more "pushback" than you expected. Could you have done better by engaging your audience and answering the difficult questions while "reacting spontaneously and naturally without hesitation and without purposeless resistance?" In my experience, when I have received challenging questions from a skeptical or even hostile or aggressive person, a natural, nonaggressive response from myself always proves more effective than showing any irritation or defensiveness. Butting heads is very easy to do, but usually leads to a sure defeat for the presenter.

Presenting Under Fire

At some point, you will encounter a hostile client or an audience member who may be more interested in making you look foolish or derailing you during your talk than getting at the truth. It happens. The key is to remember that they are never the enemy. If there is any enemy at all, it is within us. Even if an audience member does choose to assume the role of "opponent," your irritation or any display of anger will surely not do you or the rest of your audience (90% of whom may support your views) any good at all.

In the world of judo, founder Jigoro Kano had this to say about dealing with an opponent: "Victory over the opponent is achieved by giving way to the strength of the opponent, adapting to it and taking advantage of it, turning it in the end to your own advantage."

Many years ago I was giving a presentation to a large group. It was going very well, but one person in the audience often interrupted with irrelevant comments to the point of becoming a distraction for the audience. I had many occasions to become angry (but did not). I could sense that the audience felt I was going to rip into the guy if there was one more interruption. And frankly, they would not have blamed me. But I remained respectful of the man and did not show any irritation or anger (nor did I allow his interruptions to derail the talk). After the presentation, several people complimented me on my handling of the "interrupter." The ironic thing was that although the boisterous man may have intended to damage my effectiveness, he actually had the opposite influence. By flowing with the moment, not butting heads with him—which only would have made things worse—and showing self-control, I gained respect from the audience.

Contribution and Being in the Moment

Every presentation is a performance, and Ben Zander knows a thing or two about the art of performance. You may know Ben Zander as the talented conductor for the Boston Philharmonic Orchestra, but he is also one of the truly gifted presenters of our time. He's so good, in fact, so inspiring and so informative, that he could spend all his time just talking to companies and organizations about leadership and transformation. As Dan Pink and I were riding the train back to central Osaka in the spring of 2007, he tipped me off to Ben Zander. There are a lot of good presenters, Dan said, but Ben Zander is one of those gifted few who is in another league. That same day I then purchased *The Art of Possibility: Transforming Professional and Personal Life* (Penguin) by Rosamund and Benjamin Zander, and I was inspired. The suggestion to check out Ben Zander as a speaker/presenter was the best tip I have received in a very long time. Ironically, the next month I presented for a Fortune 500 company and found that every single person in the room was well-versed in the Zanders' teachings and that their simple advice had a powerful effect within their company.

Here's a sample of the kind of remarkable messages Ben Zander conveys to his audiences. In this case, he is talking in the context of musicianship, but his words can be applied to most of our presentation situations, too:

> *"This is the moment—this is the most important moment right now. Which is: We are about contribution. That's what our job is. It's not about impressing people. It's not about getting the next job. It's about contributing something."*
>
> — *Benjamin Zander*

It's not always about success or failure, it's about contribution and being fully present. Rather than asking questions such as "Will I be appreciated?" or "Will I win them over?" and so on, ask "How can I make a contribution?" Here is what Ben Zander said to a talented young musician while coaching him on his musical performance: "We are about contribution, that's what our job is… everyone was clear you contributed passion to the people in this room. Did you do it better than the next violinist, or did he do better than a pianist? I don't care, because in contribution, there is no better!"

The Zanders say that rather than getting bogged down in a sea of measurement where you compare yourself to others and worry about whether you are worthy to be making the presentation or whether someone else could be doing it better, instead realize that at this moment in time—right here right now—you are the gift, and your message is the contribution. There is no "better," there is only now. It really is pretty simple.

Not every presentation situation is about contribution, perhaps, but most are. In fact, I don't think I have ever given a presentation that was not at some level about making a contribution. Certainly, when you are asked to share your expertise with a group who are on the whole not specialists in your field, you have to think very hard about what is important (for them) and what is not (again, *for them*). It is easier just to do the same presentation you always do, but it is not about impressing people with the depths of your knowledge, it's about sharing or teaching something of lasting value.

Passion, Risk, and "Playing on One Buttock"

In most cultures—and certainly here in Japan—making a mistake is the worst thing you can do. Zander says that it's dangerous for musicians, for example, to be so concerned with competition and measuring themselves against others because this makes it "difficult to take the necessary risks with themselves to become great performers." Only through mistakes can you see where you're lacking, where you need to work. We hate mistakes, so we play it safe. Yet long term, nothing could be more dangerous if your goal is to be great at what you do. Zander suggests that instead of getting so dejected by mistakes, we should instead exclaim loudly, raising our arms (or to ourselves) "How fascinating!" every time we make a mistake. Think about that. Another mistake? How fascinating! Another opportunity to learn something just presented itself. Another unlucky break? No worries! Move forward. You cannot worry about mistakes and be fully present in the moment at the same time.

It is not enough to know a piece of music intellectually or to play it without any mistakes, you have to convey the true language of the music emotionally, says Zander. When musicians truly get into the music and play it with such heart and emotion that audiences are moved beyond words, Zander noticed that the music flows through the musicians, taking control of their bodies as they sway from side to side. Zander, then, urges musicians to become "one-buttock players," that is to let the music flow through their bodies, causing them to lean and to move from one buttock to the other. If you're a musician, or making a performance of virtually any kind, and you are totally in the moment and connecting with the language of the music and the audience, there is no way you can be a "two-buttock player." You've got to move, you've got to connect, and you must not hold back your passion but instead let the audience have a taste of the commitment, energy, and passion you have for the music (or the topic, the ideas, etc.).

You can hold back, aim not to make an error and play it perfectly "on two buttocks," or you can say "Screw it!—I'll take a risk" and dare to lean into the music with intensity, color, humanity, and passion and quite possibly, in your own small way (and on only one buttock), change the world. Play it with total sincerity and with your entire body—heart and soul—and you will make a connection and change things. As Ben Zander said while encouraging one of his talented students to play it in the "one-buttock" style: "If you play that way, they won't be able to resist you. You will be a compelling force behind which everyone will be inspired to play their best."

Don't Take Yourself So Seriously!

"Lighten up," says Zander, "and you lighten up those around you." This is not to suggest that you shouldn't take your work seriously (you should), or even that you shouldn't take yourself seriously (that may depend on time and place), but as an absolute certainty, we must all get over ourselves. There is perhaps no better way to get over ourselves than the use of humor.

Rosamund Zander, the philosopher of the partnership, says that from birth we are concerned about measurement and worried about the perceived scarcity of love, attention, food, and so on that seems to be the way of the world. She calls this the "calculating self," and in this environment of scarcity, competition, and comparison "the self needs to be taken very seriously indeed." No matter how successful and confident you may become as an adult, your "calculating self" (concerned with measurement and worried about scarcity) is weak and sees itself at risk of losing everything.

The goal, then, is to move away from the calculating self, the self that lives in a world of scarcity, exaggerated threats, and deficiencies, and move toward a healthier attitude of sufficiency, wholeness, and possibilities. Getting over yourself—and humor is a great vehicle for this—allows you to see the "creative nature of the world and ourselves." When you understand what an infant can't—that is, you cannot control the world, you cannot impose your will on people's hearts—you begin to get over yourself. When you learn to lighten up, you see yourself as permeable, not vulnerable, says Mrs. Zander, and you stay open to the unknown and to new influences, new ideas. Rather than trying to resist and fight the river of life, you move through it with a harmonious fluidity and grace, learning to join rather than resist the flow. Humor is a wonderful way to remind everyone around us—no matter how hard the work gets—that our true and most "central" self is not obsessed with childish demands, entitlements, and calculations but is instead supportive, confident, helpful, and even inspiring. A presentation is as good a time as any to let people see that side of you.

In Sum

- Like a conversation, presentation requires your full presence at that time and place.

- Like a master swordsman, you must be completely in the moment without thoughts of the past or the future, or of "winning" and "losing."

- Mistakes may happen, but do not dwell on past mistakes or worry about future ones. Be only in this moment, sharing and conversing with the audience in front of you.

- You will make it look easy and natural by preparing and practicing like mad. The more you rehearse, the more confident you'll become, and the easier it will seem to the audience.

- Though you must plan well, being fully in the moment also means that you remain flexible, totally aware, and open to the possibilities as they arise.

Connecting with an Audience

Most of what I have learned about communication and connection did not come from my speech and communication classes in school, it came from my experience as a performer and from years of closely watching others perform. I worked my way through college playing drums in various jazz groups beginning when I was 17. I don't care how technically "good" the music is, I have never seen a great performance that lacked a solid connection between the performer and the audience.

Playing music is a performance and also very much a presentation. Good presentations are about conversing, sharing, and connecting at an intellectual *and* emotional level in an honest and sincere way. It doesn't get much more honest than jazz (which has been called "the music of dialogue"). It is even easier to connect when playing music since everything is laid right out there in front for everyone to see and hear. There are no politics and no walls. The music may touch the audience or it may not, but there is never even the hint of insincerity, questionable motives, or of being anything other than what people see before them at that moment. The smiles, the heads nodding in agreement, and the feet tapping under the tables tell me that there is a connection, and that connection is no less than communication. It's a fantastic feeling.

Tom Grant, based in Portland, Oregon, is a musical legend in the U.S. Pacific Northwest, and you can buy his albums or hear his songs on jazz and soft jazz stations around the world (including here in Japan). Tom's a great musician, but what I always liked about his live performances were his warmth and his friendly, engaging style that just made the connection with the audience so much better.

Photo of Tom Grant by Owen Carey

The lesson I've learned from watching great musical performances live is that the music plus the artists' ability to convey their (musical) message and connect with the audience is what it's all about. If done well, the end result is far more than just the notes played. A true performance transcends the simple act of artists playing music and people listening. It's bigger than that.

The art of musical performance and the art of presentation share the same essence. That is, it's always about bridging the distance between artist and audience to make a real connection. If there's no connection, there can be no conversation. This is true whether you're pitching a new technology, explaining a new medical treatment, or playing at Carnegie Hall.

To Tom Grant, performance is not an exhibition—I perform, you listen. Tom clearly feels it's a two-way encounter. Here's what Tom said in an interview in *Smooth Vibes* in 2005: "There is joy in music for the player and for the receiver. I play music because it is my calling in life. I hope it conveys a joy and benevolence that people can apply to their own lives and thus improve, if only in the tiniest way, the quality of life on earth."

Are not presentations about the player (presenter) and the receiver (audience)? A good tip to always remember: It's not about us, it's about them. And about the message.

Hara Hachi Bu: Why Length Matters

A consequence of Zen practice is increased attentiveness to the present, a calmness, and a good ability to focus on the here and now. However, for your average audience member, it is a safe bet that he is not completely "calm" or completely present in the "here and now," but is instead processing many emotional opinions and juggling several issues at the moment—both professional and personal—while doing his best to listen to you. We all struggle with this. It is virtually impossible for our audience to concentrate completely on what we are saying, even for shorter presentations. Many studies show that concentration really takes a hit after 15-20 minutes. My experience tells me it's less than that. For example, CEOs have notoriously short attention spans while listening to a presentation. So the length of your presentation matters.

Every case is different, but generally, shorter is better. But why then do so many presenters go past their allotted time, or milk a presentation to stretch it out to the allotted time, even when it seems that the points have pretty much been made? This is probably a result of much of our education. I can still hear my college philosophy professor saying before the two-hour in-class written exam: "Remember, more is better." As students, we grow up in an atmosphere that perpetuates the idea that a 20-page paper will likely get a higher grade than a 10-page paper, and a one-hour presentation with 25 PowerPoint slides filled with 12pt lines of text shows more hard work than a 30-minute presentation with 50 highly visual slides. This "old school" thinking does not take into account the creativity, intellect, and forethought that it takes to achieve a clarity of ideas. We take this "more is better" thinking with us into our professional lives.

One Secret to a Healthy Life (and a Great Presentation)

The Japanese have a great expression concerning healthy eating habits: *hara hachi bu* which means "eat until 80 percent full." This is excellent advice, and it's pretty easy to follow this principle in Japan since portions are generally much smaller than in places like the U.S. Using chopsticks also makes it easier to avoid shoveling food in and encourages a bit of a slower pace. This principle does not encourage wastefulness, it does not mean to leave 20 percent of your meal on the plate. In fact, it is bad form to leave food on your plate. In Japan, and in Asia in general, we usually order as a group and then take only what we need from the shared bounty in front of us. I have found—ironically perhaps— that if I stop eating before getting full I am more satisfied with the meal, I'm not sleepy after lunch or dinner, and I just generally feel much better.

Hara hachi bu is also a principle that can be applied to the length of speeches, presentations, and even meetings. My advice is this: no matter how much time you are given, never ever go over time, and in fact finish a bit before your allotted time is up. How long you go will depend on your own unique situation at the time, but try to shoot for 90–95 percent of your allotted time. No one will complain if you finish with a few minutes to spare. The problem with most presentations is that they are too long, not that they are too short.

Leave Them Just a Little Hungry (for More)

Professional entertainers know that you want to end on a high note and leave the audience yearning for just a bit more from you. We want to leave our audiences satisfied (motivated, inspired, more knowledgeable, etc.), but not feeling that they could have done with just a little less.

We can apply this spirit to the length and amount of material we put into a presentation as well. Give them high quality—the highest you can—but do not give them so much quantity that you leave them with their heads spinning and guts aching.

This is a typical ekiben (special boxed meal sold at train stations) from one of my trips to Tokyo. Simple. Appealing. Economic in scale. Nothing superfluous. Made with the "honorable passenger" in mind. After spending 20–30 minutes savoring the contents of the bento, complemented by Japanese beer, I'm left happy, nourished, and satisfied, but not full. I could eat more—another bento perhaps—but I do not need to. Indeed, I do not want to. I am satisfied with the experience; eating to the point of becoming full would only destroy the quality of the experience I'm having.

Removing Barriers to Communication

I'm not a fan of the lectern (also referred to as the podium). Yes, it has its place, and sometimes its use is unavoidable. But in almost every speaking situation, standing behind a lectern is like standing behind a wall.

Lecterns can make a speaker look authoritative and in command. This is why politicians love speaking from behind them in most cases. If you are aiming to look "large and in charge," then perhaps a lectern is appropriate for you. But for most of us—conference presenters, lecturers, sales reps, etc.—the last place we want to be is behind a wall. Also, lecterns are often placed to the side and back from the edge of the stage. In this case, you are not only behind a barrier, your slides (if you use any) are the main focus and your physical presence is now very much playing second fiddle. It's possible for both you and the screen to be front and center, which is where people are naturally going to focus their attention.

If you present from behind a lectern, you may, more or less, sound the same and the media may look the same, but it's not ideal. Far from it. The connection is lost. Imagine if your favorite singer performed from behind a lectern. Ridiculous, of course. Imagine, too, if Steve Jobs gave keynotes with the same slides and same video clips, same jeans and black turtleneck, but did all the talking from behind a lectern. He might *sound* the same. The visuals might *look* the same. But the connection would not be there. A connection with the audience is not a sufficient condition, but it's a necessary one.

Recently, I attended a Toastmasters' speech contest in Japan. Toastmasters is rather traditional, you may be thinking. However, I found it very interesting that not one of the contestants spoke from the lectern, not a single person. All speakers placed themselves front and center (inches from the edge of the stage) and gave excellent talks, many of them moving slowly to different sides of the stage as they spoke, connecting with the whole audience.

Generally, the lectern is "so last millennium." There are times when the use of a lectern is perfectly acceptable, such as when you are one of many speakers taking their turn at the center stage at a formal ceremony. But in cases where the people have walked in that room specifically to hear you, to learn from you, to be convinced or inspired by you, then you've got to do whatever you can to remove all walls—literally and figuratively—between you and the audience. It's scary. It takes practice. But it's worth it.

If Your Idea is Worth Spreading...

I absolutely love TED (Technology, Entertainment, Design). The annual TED conference brings together the world's most fascinating thinkers and doers, who are invited to give insanely great talks on stage in only 18 minutes. The time limitation usually results in presenters making very concise, tight, and focused talks. If you're going to have ideas worth talking about then you've got to be able to stand, deliver, and make your case. As the presenters at TED demonstrate every year, presentation skill is critically important.

What's great about TED is that they don't keep their amazing presentations accessible to only an elite few. Instead, they "give it away" by uploading loads of their best presentations to the Web and make the videos available in many different formats for online viewing or download. (I watch many of the presentations on my iPod while commuting on the subway in the mornings.) Over 150 talks from the TED archive are now available, with more added each week. The production quality is excellent and so is the content. TED truly exemplifies the spirit of the conceptual age: share, give it away, make it easy, because the more people who know your idea, the more powerful it becomes. Because of the high-quality free videos, the reach and impact of TED has been huge. The TED Web site is a great resource.

www.ted.com/talks

Stand, Deliver, Connect

Hans Rosling (right), a professor of global health at Sweden's Karolinska Institute, is the Zen master of presenting statistics that have meaning and  tell a story. Rosling co-developed the software behind his visualizations through his nonprofit Gapminder. Using UN statistics, Rosling shows that it is indeed a different world. You can see two presentations on the TED Web site that show Rosling's talents. Conventional wisdom says never stand between the screen and the projector. Generally this is good advice. But as you can see from the photo here, Rosling at times defies conventional wisdom and gets involved with the data in an energetic way that engages his audience with the data and his story.

The TED presenters on this page demonstrate the importance of standing front and center and connecting with the audience.

Hans Rosling (*TED/ leslieimage.com*)

June Cohen
(*TED/ leslieimage.com*)

John Doerr
(*TED/ leslieimage.com*)

Lawrence Lessig
(*TED/ leslieimage.com*)

Carolyn Porco
(*TED/ leslieimage.com*)

Keep the Lights On

It is a common reaction all over the world: Just as the presenter is ready to begin, someone shouts "could you get the lights, please!" And the room becomes shrouded in darkness, save for the light reflecting off the screen. The presenter? She must be there somewhere, I can hear her speaking (or is that the audience breathing?).

If you want your presentation to be more effective, then don't touch that light switch. Even when you are using slides, the more lights you can keep on, the better off you will be. Remember, you're trying to connect, to tell a story, to sell an idea to the board or other decision makers. It is very difficult to make a connection if the audience can't *see* you. The audience is not there to witness the narration of slides; they are there to listen to you and become engaged with you and your topic. If the audience can't see you, they will find it difficult to listen, and they are certainly more likely to tune you out.

The audience must experience both your "verbal speech" and your "visual speech." A relatively small part of your message is actually verbal. The rest of your message is expressed visually and vocally. Influencing people verbally becomes far more difficult when they can't see you.

Cliff Atkinson reminds us of the evidence that supports the claim that the more the audience can both see and hear you, the better. "It turns out that when you watch people speak, the visual cues help you to predict and understand the auditory cues that follow soon after. These visual cues are actually not limited to the lips, but include the entire human face," says Atkinson. According to the authors of *Why Business People Speak like Idiots* (Free Press), "...human beings are hard-wired to draw much more meaning from people than they are from the information that people present." True, but they've got to *see* you.

Ten years ago, projectors were not all that bright, so turning the lights off made more sense. Today, even inexpensive business projectors are usually bright enough for a smaller venue or teaching situation. There is no good reason for turning off all the lights today in most situations. In many cases, you just have to compromise. The slides may look better with all the lights off, but you'll disappear. With all the lights on, the screen may wash out completely. In this case, you can dim just the lights in front if possible. Look for a balance, but do not present in the dark.

In corporate meeting rooms across Japan, common practice is to turn all or most of the lights off for presentations. It is also very common for the presenter to sit on the side or back of the table operating the PC while the audience stares at the screen as the "presenter" narrates the slides. This practice is so common that it is considered "normal." It may be normal, but it is not effective. Audiences will better understand the presenter's message when they can both hear *and see* the presenter.

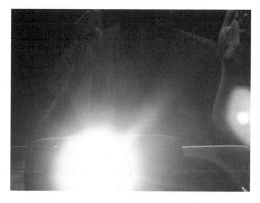

Remote Simplicity: Use a Small Remote to Advance Slides

I see a lot of presentations by very smart people, yet all too often the presenter either uses a remote poorly (as if it is the first time he's seen such a device) or does not use a remote at all. Even today, too many presenters stay next to the computer on a table or lectern or walk back to the computer to change slides every few minutes.

Remote control devices for computers are relatively cheap and an absolute must. No excuses, you've got to have one. If you are not currently using a remote to advance slides, adding a remote to your delivery style will make a huge difference. The remote allows you to get out front closer to the people, to move to different parts of the stage or room, and to make those connections.

When we stay glued to the laptop and look down to advance every slide, our presentations become more like slide shows with narration, the kind our uncle used to bore us with when he whipped out his 35mm slide projector with highlights of his latest fishing trip. Yawn.

Remember, you want the technology behind your presentation to be as invisible as possible to the audience. But when you have your hand on the computer and your eyes are moving back and forth from the computer screen, to the keyboard, to the audience (or projection screen), this becomes more like the typical PowerPoint presentation that people complain about.

Small and basic is all you need. I prefer small remotes with only the most basic features. You can buy remotes that you can mouse around with on-screen and are equipped with myriad other features, but they are large and call attention to themselves. All I really need is the ability to advance, go back, and turn the screen black. Very simple.

In Sum

- You need solid content and logical structure, but you also have to make a connection with the audience. You must appeal to both the logical and the emotional.

- If your content is worth talking about, then bring energy and passion to your delivery. Every situation is different, but there is never an excuse for being dull.

- Don't hold back. If you have a passion for your topic, then let people know it.

- Remember *hara hachi bu.* It is better to leave your audience satisfied yet yearning for a bit more of you than it is to leave your audience stuffed and feeling that they have had more than enough.

- Keep the lights on; the audience must always be able to see you.

- Remove any barriers between you and the audience. Avoid podiums (lecterns), if possible. And use a wireless mic and remote control for advancing slides so that you can move around freely and naturally.

next step

What we think, we become.

—Buddha

10

The Journey Begins

Many people look for the short road and the quick fix to achieve presentation excellence. But it doesn't exist: there are no panaceas or off-the-shelf fixes. Learning to become an exceptional presenter in today's world is a journey. In this journey, there are many paths to presenting in a more "enlightened" way, a way that is appropriate for the world in which we live. The first step down the road to becoming a great presenter is simply seeing—really seeing—that that which passes for normal and ordinary and good enough is off-kilter with how we learn, understand, remember, and engage.

No matter what your starting point is today, you can become much better. In fact, you can become extraordinary. I know this is true because I have seen it many times before. I have worked with professionals—young and old—who believed that they were not particularly creative, charismatic, or dynamic, and yet with a little help they were able to transform themselves into extremely creative, highly articulate, engaging presenters once they realized that that person—that remarkable presenter—was in them already. Once they opened their eyes and made the commitment to learn and leave the past behind, it was just a matter of time before great progress was visible. Interestingly, as their confidence grew and they became more effective presenters, their newly found confidence and perspective had a remarkable impact on other aspects of their personal and professional lives.

How to Improve

There are many things you can do to become a better presenter (with or without the use of multimedia) and a better, more effective communicator in general. Here are just a few things to keep in mind.

Read and Study

Through books, DVDs, and myriad online resources, you can teach yourself much of what is needed to be an exceptional presenter. I list over 75 books, DVDs, and Web sites on the Presentation Zen Web site (presentationzen.com) which are related to presentation design and delivery. Most of the items I recommend are not necessarily about presentation skills or slideware at all. However, these are the resources that are often the most helpful. For example, you can learn a lot about storytelling and the use of imagery by studying the masters of documentary film and cinema. Even books on writing screen plays will teach you lessons you can apply to the world of presentations. You just never know what you'll learn through self-study, especially when you look in unusual places.

Just Do It

Reading and studying are important and necessary, but to really get better at presentations—including the design of visuals—you have to actually *do it,* and do it often. So look for opportunities to present. If there is a local Toastmasters (*www.toastmasters.org*) chapter in your area, consider getting involved. You'll not only get many opportunities to speak and present with Toastmasters, but you'll also expand your network and make new friends, all of whom have an interest in mastering public speaking. Volunteer to present for your school, business, or civic group, and look for opportunities to "give it away."

Finding inspiration in jazz...

Exercise Your "Right Brain"

It is important for working professionals—no matter what their field is—to stay in touch with their "creative soul" and to nurture it. What a waste it would be to ignore one of your passions or talents. Frankly, you just never know where inspiration will come from. Inspiration, clarity, or a new perspective may materialize unforced as you climb that mountain, paint that portrait, photograph that sunset, write that novel... or find that "pocket" while playing with fellow musicians in a downtown nightclub.

...and the blues...

I no longer play music fulltime, but I still perform from time to time with local jazz musicians or blues bands in Japan. It's so good for the creative soul to play live and connect with other musicians and an audience. Blues especially is about connecting and telling a story through the words and music. It's about feelings. Playing the blues well is similar to making great presentations: it's not about technique. Once you begin to focus on technique and tricks and flash and making an impression, all is lost. If I never played music I would miss all the lessons.

Get Out

Nothing great will ever happen to you if you stay in your comfort zone. So as much as you can, get out of your office or school or house and make connections and look to exercise the right side of your brain. "Out there" is where the learning occurs. Challenge yourself and develop your creativity; exercise your creative brain. Take a drama class. Take an art class. Go to a movie. Go to a concert. Go to a play or a musical. If you're a musician, join an orchestra or jam with friends or form a band. Or just go for an inspirational walk alone.

...or visiting a temple in Kyoto.

Lessons Are All Around You

We can find inspiration and lessons in unexpected places. For example, over the years I've learned a lot about graphic design—what's effective and what's not—during the morning commute on the trains. Trains here in Japan are clean, comfortable, and on time. The trains are also full of print advertising hanging and affixed to every conceivable space. I enjoy scanning the print ads while I commute as this gives me a chance to keep abreast of new products and events, and also to study graphic design trends and observe the way graphics and print are used in the media.  You can learn a lot about fundamental design principles and develop a critical eye through careful examination of graphic design found in posters, banners, street signs, store fronts, and so on. We usually ignore or take for granted so much of the design in an urban setting, but just walking down the street you'll find that the examples from which to learn are all around you. The lessons are everywhere. It's just a matter of seeing.

It's Within You Already

The key is in knowing that it is within you already. Do not rely on Microsoft or Apple or anyone else to dictate your choices. Most of all, do not let mere habit—and the habits of others—dictate your decisions on how you prepare and design and ultimately deliver your presentations. The secret is in increased awareness and being able to see the world and all the lessons around you. We cannot truly move forward and learn the new if we cling to the old. The essential key to improvement is simply having an open mind, an open heart, and a willingness to learn and even to make mistakes in the process. There are many ways to improve and transform yourself. In this chapter, I have listed just a few that I hope will be of help to you.

Conclusion

So, what's the conclusion? The conclusion is there is no conclusion, there is only the next step. And that next step is completely up to you. In fact, far from being the conclusion, for many this is just the beginning. In this book I have tried to give you a few simple things to think about as you work toward improving your presentation preparation, design, and delivery skills. This book focused on presenting while using slideware such as PowerPoint or Keynote, yet the use of multimedia technology is not appropriate for every case. You decide. But if you *do* use slideware in your next talk, aim to design and deliver your presentation while allowing the principles of restraint, simplicity, and naturalness to be your gentle guide. Enjoy the journey.

A journey of a thousand miles
begins with a single step.

—Lao-tzu

Photo Credits

Markuz Wernli Saito

Garden photographs reprinted with permission from the book *Mirei Shigemori, Modernizing The Japanese Garden* (Stone Bridge Press) by Christian Tschumi and Markuz Wernli Saito. See Markuz's portfolio at www.markuz.com.

Chapter 1

| istockphoto.com 000003332520 | istockphoto.com 000003223474 | istockphoto.com 000003405715 | istockphoto.com 000003074097 | istockphoto.com 000002928039 | istockphoto.com 000003719838 | istockphoto.com 2913656 | istockphoto.com 000003502193 |

Chapter 2   Chapter 3

| istockphoto.com 000001231803 | istockphoto.com 000003995270 | istockphoto.com 3879802 | istockphoto.com 000001271636 | istockphoto.com 000002783526 | istockphoto.com 000001101493 | istockphoto.com 000000252654 | istockphoto.com 000000252654 |

| istockphoto.com 000000825429 | istockphoto.com 000003279975 | istockphoto.com 000002844158 | istockphoto.com 000000659586 | istockphoto.com 000002807562 | istockphoto.com 000002807562 | istockphoto.com 000002761192 | istockphoto.com 000003413016 |

Chapter 4   Chapter 5

| istockphoto.com 000000210474 | istockphoto.com 000003004014 | istockphoto.com 000003080483 | istockphoto.com 000000407292 | istockphoto.com 000003083414 | istockphoto.com 000003882213 | istockphoto.com 000003386899 | istockphoto.com 000003315303 |

Chapter 6

| istockphoto.com 000001478718 | istockphoto.com 000003919934 | istockphoto.com 000002783526 | istockphoto.com 000003112172 | istockphoto.com 000002295948 | istockphoto.com 000003585072 | istockphoto.com 000002743609 |

The iStockphoto images that appear on these pages were used to enhance the presentation of the book. You can find the exact photo at iStockphoto.com by conducting a search using the unique number code for the image.

Chapter 7

istockphoto.com
000003492393

istockphoto.com
000000761342

Chapter 8

istockphoto.com
000003492393

istockphoto.com
000000761342

istockphoto.com
000002___804

istockphoto.com
000000329345

istockphoto.com
000002677242

Chapter 9

istockphoto.com
000002415000

istockphoto.com
000000071701

istockphoto.com
000002699219

istockphoto.com
000003685771

Chapter 10

istockphoto.com
000001067505

istockphoto.com
000003216945X

istockphoto.com
000004344227

Cover photo

by Alex Bramwell
istockphoto.com
000003043850

Index

Colophon

This book was written and designed entirely on a 15-inch Apple MacBook Pro with a 2.33 GHz Intel Core Duo processor and 2 GB of RAM. Some of the early writing took place while I balanced the MacBook on my lap on the beach in both Oregon and Hawaii; most of the writing took place in the Hommachi Starbucks in downtown Osaka, Japan. The text was written in Microsoft Word, and after editing, was placed in Adobe InDesign. InDesign was used for all layout and design of the book's interior. Adobe Illustrator was used to create the front and back covers.

For the design work I connected a 20-inch Apple Cinema Display to the MacBook in my home office to give me dual monitors and enough space to work on the layout. Adobe InDesign was used for all layout work. Most of the slides were created in Apple's Keynote (and Microsoft's PowerPoint) and then exported as TIFF images for the book. Adobe Photoshop was used to edit all photo images, including changing all the photos and slide images from RGB to CMYK for printing.

Helvetica was used for the book's title. Gill Sans was used for the back cover. Gill Sans was also used in the book' s interior for sidebars, callouts, and some titles. Trade Gothic was used for the main body text and some titles.

OUR IMAGE
YOUR STORY